Complete Poems of
Frances E. W. Harper

THE SCHOMBURG LIBRARY OF
NINETEENTH-CENTURY BLACK WOMEN WRITERS

General Editor, Henry Louis Gates, Jr.

Titles are listed chronologically; collections that include works published over a span of years are listed according to the publication date of their initial work.

Complete Poems

of

Frances E. W. Harper

Edited by
MARYEMMA GRAHAM

New York   Oxford
OXFORD UNIVERSITY PRESS
1988

Oxford University Press

Oxford   New York   Toronto
Delhi   Bombay   Calcutta   Madras   Karachi
Petaling Jaya   Singapore   Hong Kong   Tokyo
Nairobi   Dar es Salaam   Cape Town
Melbourne   Auckland

and associated companies in
Beirut   Berlin   Ibadan   Nicosia

Library of Congress Cataloging-in-Publication Data

Harper, Frances Ellen Watkins, 1825–1911.
[Poems]
Complete poems of Frances E. W. Harper/ edited by Maryemma Graham.
p. cm.—(The Schomburg library of nineteenth-century black
women writers)
I. Graham, Maryemma.   II. Title.   III. Series.
PS1799.H7A17   1988   811'.3—dc19   87-24073
ISBN 0-19-505244-7
ISBN 0-19-505267-6 (set)

6 8 10 9 7 5
Printed in the United States of America
on acid-free paper

The
Schomburg Library
of
Nineteenth-Century
Black Women Writers
is
Dedicated
in Memory
of
PAULINE AUGUSTA COLEMAN GATES

1916–1987

PUBLISHER'S NOTE

FOREWORD
In Her Own Write

Henry Louis Gates, Jr.

One muffled strain in the Silent South, a jarring chord and a
vague and uncomprehended cadenza has been and still is the
Negro. And of that muffled chord, the one mute and voiceless note has been the sadly expectant Black Woman, ...

The "other side" has not been represented by one who "lives
there." And not many can more sensibly realize and more
accurately tell the weight and the fret of the "long dull pain"
than the open-eyed but hitherto voiceless Black Woman of
America.

. . . as our Caucasian barristers are not to blame if they
cannot *quite* put themselves in the dark man's place, neither
should the dark man be wholly expected fully and adequately
to reproduce the exact Voice of the Black Woman.

    —ANNA JULIA COOPER, *A Voice From the South* (1892)

The birth of the Afro-American literary tradition occurred
in 1773, when Phillis Wheatley published a book of poetry.
Despite the fact that her book garnered for her a remarkable
amount of attention, Wheatley's journey to the printer had
been a most arduous one. Sometime in 1772, a young African girl walked demurely into a room in Boston to undergo
an oral examination, the results of which would determine
the direction of her life and work. Perhaps she was shocked
upon entering the appointed room. For there, perhaps gath-

ered in a semicircle, sat eighteen of Boston's most notable citizens. Among them were John Erving, a prominent Boston merchant; the Reverend Charles Chauncy, pastor of the Tenth Congregational Church; and John Hancock, who would later gain fame for his signature on the Declaration of Independence. At the center of this group was His Excellency, Thomas Hutchinson, governor of Massachusetts, with Andrew Oliver, his lieutenant governor, close by his side.

Why had this august group been assembled? Why had it seen fit to summon this young African girl, scarcely eighteen years old, before it? This group of "the most respectable Characters in *Boston*," as it would later define itself, had assembled to question closely the African adolescent on the slender sheaf of poems that she claimed to have "written by herself." We can only speculate on the nature of the questions posed to the fledgling poet. Perhaps they asked her to identify and explain—for all to hear—exactly who were the Greek and Latin gods and poets alluded to so frequently in her work. Perhaps they asked her to conjugate a verb in Latin or even to translate randomly selected passages from the Latin, which she and her master, John Wheatley, claimed that she "had made some Progress in." Or perhaps they asked her to recite from memory key passages from the texts of John Milton and Alexander Pope, the two poets by whom the African claimed to be most directly influenced. We do not know.

We do know, however, that the African poet's responses were more than sufficient to prompt the eighteen august gentlemen to compose, sign, and publish a two-paragraph "Attestation," an open letter "To the Publick" that prefaces Phillis Wheatley's book and that reads in part:

> We whose Names are under-written, do assure the World, that the Poems specified in the following Page, were (as we

verily believe) written by Phillis, a young Negro Girl, who was but a few Years since, brought an uncultivated Barbarian from *Africa*, and has ever since been, and now is, under the Disadvantage of serving as a Slave in a Family in this Town. She has been examined by some of the best Judges, and is thought qualified to write them.

So important was this document in securing a publisher for Wheatley's poems that it forms the signal element in the prefatory matter preceding her *Poems on Various Subjects, Religious and Moral,* published in London in 1773.

Without the published "Attestation," Wheatley's publisher claimed, few would believe that an African could possibly have written poetry all by herself. As the eighteen put the matter clearly in their letter, "Numbers would be ready to suspect they were not really the Writings of Phillis." Wheatley and her master, John Wheatley, had attempted to publish a similar volume in 1772 in Boston, but Boston publishers had been incredulous. One year later, "Attestation" in hand, Phillis Wheatley and her master's son, Nathaniel Wheatley, sailed for England, where they completed arrangements for the publication of a volume of her poems with the aid of the Countess of Huntington and the Earl of Dartmouth.

This curious anecdote, surely one of the oddest oral examinations on record, is only a tiny part of a larger, and even more curious, episode in the Enlightenment. Since the beginning of the sixteenth century, Europeans had wondered aloud whether or not the African "species of men," as they were most commonly called, *could* ever create formal literature, could ever master "the arts and sciences." If they could, the argument ran, then the African variety of humanity was fundamentally related to the European variety. If not, then it seemed clear that the African was destined by nature

to be a slave. This was the burden shouldered by Phillis
Wheatley when she successfully defended herself and the au-
thorship of her book against counterclaims and doubts.

Indeed, with her successful defense, Wheatley launched
two traditions at once—the black American literary tradition
and the black woman's literary tradition. If it is extraordinary
that not just one but both of these traditions were founded
simultaneously by a black woman—certainly an event unique
in the history of literature—it is also ironic that this important fact of common, coterminous literary origins seems to
have escaped most scholars.

That the progenitor of the black literary tradition was a
woman means, in the most strictly literal sense, that all subsequent black writers have evolved in a matrilinear line of
descent, and that each, consciously or unconsciously, has extended and revised a canon whose foundation was the poetry
of a black woman. Early black writers seem to have been
keenly aware of Wheatley's founding role, even if most of
her white reviewers were more concerned with the implica-
tions of her race than her gender. Jupiter Hammon, for example, whose 1760 broadside "An Evening Thought. Salvation by Christ, With Penitential Cries" was the first
individual poem published by a black American, acknowl-
edged Wheatley's influence by selecting her as the subject of
his second broadside, "An Address to Miss Phillis Wheatly
[*sic*], Ethiopian Poetess, in Boston," which was published at
Hartford in 1778. And George Moses Horton, the second
Afro-American to publish a book of poetry in English (1829),
brought out in 1838 an edition of his *Poems By A Slave*
bound together with Wheatley's work. Indeed, for fifty-six
years, between 1773 and 1829, when Horton published *The
Hope of Liberty*, Wheatley was the *only* black person to have
published a book of imaginative literature in English. So

central was this black woman's role in the shaping of the Afro-American literary tradition that, as one historian has maintained, the history of the reception of Phillis Wheatley's poetry *is* the history of Afro-American literary criticism. Well into the nineteenth century, Wheatley and the black literary tradition were the same entity.

But Wheatley is not the only black woman writer who stands as a pioneering figure in Afro-American literature. Just as Wheatley gave birth to the genre of black poetry, Ann Plato was the first Afro-American to publish a book of essays (1841) and Harriet E. Wilson was the first black person to publish a novel in the United States (1859).

Despite this pioneering role of black women in the tradition, however, many of their contributions before this century have been all but lost or unrecognized. As Hortense Spillers observed as recently as 1983,

> With the exception of a handful of autobiographical narratives from the nineteenth century, the black woman's realities are virtually suppressed until the period of the Harlem Renaissance and later. Essentially the black woman as artist, as intellectual spokesperson for her own cultural apprenticeship, has not existed before, for anyone. At the source of [their] own symbol-making task, [the community of black women writers] confronts, therefore, a tradition of work that is quite recent, its continuities, broken and sporadic.

Until now, it has been extraordinarily difficult to establish the formal connections between early black women's writing and that of the present, precisely because our knowledge of their work has been broken and sporadic. Phillis Wheatley, for example, while certainly the most reprinted and discussed poet in the tradition, is also one of the least understood. Ann Plato's seminal work, *Essays* (which includes biographies and poems), has not been reprinted since it was published a cen-

tury and a half ago. And Harriet Wilson's *Our Nig,* her
compelling novel of a black woman's expanding consciousness in a racist Northern antebellum environment, never received even *one* review or comment at a time when virtually
all works written by black people were heralded by abolition-
ists as salient arguments against the existence of human slavery. Many of the books reprinted in this set experienced a
similar fate, the most dreadful fate for an author: that of
being ignored then relegated to the obscurity of the rare book
section of a university library. We can only wonder how
many other texts in the black woman's tradition have been
lost to this generation of readers or remain unclassified or
uncatalogued and, hence, unread.

This was not always so, however. Black women writers
dominated the final decade of the nineteenth century, perhaps
spurred to publish by an 1886 essay entitled "The Coming
American Novelist," which was published in *Lippincott's
Monthly Magazine* and written by "A Lady From Philadelphia." This pseudonymous essay argued that the "Great
American Novel" would be written by a black person. Her
argument is so curious that it deserves to be repeated:

> When we come to formulate our demands of the Coming
> American Novelist, we will agree that he must be native-
> born. His ancestors may come from where they will, but we
> must give him a birthplace and have the raising of him. Still,
> the longer his family has been here the better he will represent
> us. Suppose he should have no country but ours, no traditions
> but those he has learned here, no longings apart from us, no
> future except in our future—the orphan of the world, he
> finds with us his home. And with all this, suppose he refuses
> to be fused into that grand conglomerate we call the "Amer-
> ican type." With us, he is not of us. He is original, he has
> humor, he is tender, he is passive and fiery, he has been

taught what we call justice, and he has his own opinion about it. He has suffered everything a poet, a dramatist, a novelist need suffer before he comes to have his lips anointed. And with it all he is in one sense a spectator, a little out of the race. How would these conditions go towards forming an original development? In a word, suppose the coming novelist is of African origin? When one comes to consider the subject, there is no improbability in it. One thing is certain,—our great novel will not be written by the typical American.

An atypical American, indeed. Not only would the great American novel be written by an African-American, it would be written by an African-American *woman:*

Yet farther: I have used the generic masculine pronoun because it is convenient; but Fate keeps revenge in store. It was a woman who, taking the wrongs of the African as her theme, wrote the novel that awakened the world to their reality, and why should not the coming novelist be a woman as well as an African? She—the woman of that race—has some claims on Fate which are not yet paid up.

It is these claims on fate that we seek to pay by publishing The Schomburg Library of Nineteenth-Century Black Women Writers.

This theme would be repeated by several black women authors, most notably by Anna Julia Cooper, a prototypical black feminist whose 1892 *A Voice From the South* can be considered to be one of the original texts of the black feminist movement. It was Cooper who first analyzed the fallacy of referring to "the Black man" when speaking of black people and who argued that just as white men cannot speak through the consciousness of black men, neither can black *men* "fully and adequately . . . reproduce the exact Voice of the Black Woman." Gender and race, she argues, cannot be conflated, except in the instance of a black woman's voice, and it is this voice which must be uttered and to which we must listen. As Cooper puts the matter so compellingly:

> It is not the intelligent woman vs. the ignorant woman; nor the white woman vs. the black, the brown, and the red,—it is not even the cause of woman vs. man. Nay, 'tis woman's strongest vindication for speaking that *the world needs to hear her voice.* It would be subversive of every human interest that the cry of one-half the human family be stifled. Woman in stepping from the pedestal of statue-like inactivity in the domestic shrine, and daring to think and move and speak,— to undertake to help shape, mold, and direct the thought of her age, is merely completing the circle of the world's vision. Hers is every interest that has lacked an interpreter and a defender. Her cause is linked with that of every agony that has been dumb—every wrong that needs a voice.
>
> It is no fault of man's that he has not been able to see truth from her standpoint. It does credit both to his head and heart that no greater mistakes have been committed or even wrongs perpetrated while she sat making tatting and snipping paper flowers. Man's own innate chivalry and the mutual interdependence of their interests have insured his treating her cause, in the main at least, as his own. And he is pardonably surprised and even a little chagrined, perhaps, to find his legislation not considered "perfectly lovely" in every respect. But in any case his work is only impoverished by her remaining dumb. The world has had to limp along with the wobbling gait and one-sided hesitancy of a man with one eye. Suddenly the bandage is removed from the other eye and the whole body is filled with light. It sees a circle where before it saw a segment. The darkened eye restored, every member rejoices with it.

The myopic sight of the darkened eye can only be restored when the full range of the black woman's voice, with its own special timbres and shadings, remains mute no longer.

Similarly, Victoria Earle Matthews, an author of short stories and essays, and a cofounder in 1896 of the National Association of Colored Women, wrote in her stunning essay, "The Value of Race Literature" (1895), that "when the literature of our race is developed, it will of necessity be different in all essential points of greatness, true heroism and real Christianity from what we may at the present time, for convenience, call American literature." Matthews argued that this great tradition of Afro-American literature would be the textual outlet "for the unnaturally suppressed inner lives which our people have been compelled to lead." Once these "unnaturally suppressed inner lives" of black people are unveiled, no "grander diffusion of mental light" will shine more brightly, she concludes, than that of the articulate Afro-American woman:

And now comes the question, What part shall we women play in the Race Literature of the future? . . . within the compass of one small journal ["Woman's Era"] we have struck out a new line of departure—a journal, a record of Race interests gathered from all parts of the United States, carefully selected, moistened, winnowed and garnered by the ablest intellects of educated colored women, shrinking at no lofty theme, shirking no serious duty, aiming at every possible excellence, and determined to do their part in the future uplifting of the race.

If twenty women, by their concentrated efforts in one literary movement, can meet with such success as has engendered, planned out, and so successfully consummated this convention, what much more glorious results, what wider spread success, what grander diffusion of mental light will not come forth at the bidding of the enlarged hosts of women writers, already called into being by the stimulus of your efforts?

And here let me speak one word for my journalistic sisters

who have already entered the broad arena of journalism. Before the "Woman's Era" had come into existence, no one except themselves can appreciate the bitter experience and sore disappointments under which they have at all times been compelled to pursue their chosen vocations.

If their brothers of the press have had their difficulties to contend with, I am here as a sister journalist to state, from the fullness of knowledge, that their task has been an easy one compared with that of the colored woman in journalism.

Woman's part in Race Literature, as in Race building, is the most important part and has been so in all ages. . . . All through the most remote epochs she has done her share in literature. . . .

One of the most important aspects of this set is the republication of the salient texts from 1890 to 1910, which literary historians could well call "The Black Woman's Era." In addition to Mary Helen Washington's definitive edition of Cooper's *A Voice From the South*, we have reprinted two novels by Amelia Johnson, Frances Harper's *Iola Leroy*, two novels by Emma Dunham Kelley, Alice Dunbar-Nelson's two impressive collections of short stories, and Pauline Hopkins's three serialized novels as well as her monumental novel, *Contending Forces*—all published between 1890 and 1910. Indeed, black women published more works of fiction in these two decades than black men had published in the previous half century. Nevertheless, this great achievement has been ignored.

Moreover, the writings of nineteenth-century Afro-American women in general have remained buried in obscurity, accessible only in research libraries or in overpriced and poorly edited reprints. Many of these books have never been reprinted at all; in some instances only one or two copies are extant. In these works of fiction, poetry, autobiography, bi-

ography, essays, and journalism resides the mind of the
nineteenth-century Afro-American woman. Until these works
are made readily available to teachers and their students, a
significant segment of the black tradition will remain silent.

Oxford University Press, in collaboration with the Schomburg Center for Research in Black Culture, is publishing
thirty volumes of these compelling works, each of which
contains an introduction by an expert in the field. The set
includes such rare texts as Johnson's *The Hazeley Family* and
Clarence and Corinne, Plato's *Essays*, the most complete edition of Phillis Wheatley's poems and letters, Emma Dunham
Kelley's pioneering novel *Megda*, several previously unpublished stories and a novel by Alice Dunbar-Nelson, and the
first collected volumes of Pauline Hopkins's three serialized
novels and Frances Harper's poetry. We also present four
volumes of poetry by such women as Mary Eliza Tucker
Lambert, Adah Menken, Josephine Heard, and Maggie
Johnson. Numerous slave and spiritual narratives, a newly
discovered novel—*Four Girls at Cottage City*—by Emma
Dunham Kelley (-Hawkins), and the first American edition
of *Wonderful Adventures of Mrs. Seacole in Many Lands* are
also among the texts included.

In addition to resurrecting the works of black women au-
thors, it is our hope that this set will facilitate the resurrection of the Afro-American woman's literary tradition itself
by unearthing its nineteenth-century roots. In the works of
Nella Larsen and Jessie Fauset, Zora Neale Hurston and Ann
Petry, Lorraine Hansberry and Gwendolyn Brooks, Paule
Marshall and Toni Cade Bambara, Audre Lorde and Rita
Dove, Toni Morrison and Alice Walker, Gloria Naylor and
Jamaica Kincaid, these roots have branched luxuriantly. The
eighteenth- and nineteenth-century authors whose works are
presented in this set founded and nurtured the black wom-

en's literary tradition, which must be revived, explicated, analyzed, and debated before we can understand more completely the formal shaping of this tradition within a tradition, a coded literary universe through which, regrettably, we are only just beginning to navigate our way. As Anna Cooper said nearly one hundred years ago, we have been blinded by the loss of sight in one eye and have therefore been unable to detect the full *shape* of the Afro-American literary tradition.

Literary works configure into a tradition not because of some mystical collective unconscious determined by the biology of race or gender, but because writers read other writers and *ground* their representations of experience in models of language provided largely by other writers to whom they feel akin. It is through this mode of literary revision, amply evident in the *texts* themselves—in formal echoes, recast metaphors, even in parody—that a "tradition" emerges and defines itself.

This is formal bonding, and it is only through formal bonding that we can know a literary tradition. The collective publication of these works by black women now, for the first time, makes it possible for scholars and critics, male and female, black and white, to *demonstrate* that black women writers read, and revised, other black women writers. To demonstrate this set of formal literary relations is to demonstrate that sexuality, race, and gender are both the condition and the basis of *tradition*—but tradition as found in discrete acts of language use.

A word is in order about the history of this set. For the past decade, I have taught a course, first at Yale and then at Cornell, entitled "Black Women and Their Fictions," a course that I inherited from Toni Morrison, who developed it in

the mid-1970s for Yale's Program in Afro-American Studies. Although the course was inspired by the remarkable ac-
complishments of black women novelists since 1970, I grad-
ually extended its beginning date to the late nineteenth century,
studying Frances Harper's *Iola Leroy* and Anna Julia Cooper's *A Voice From the South*, both published in 1892. With
the discovery of Harriet E. Wilson's seminal novel, *Our Nig*
(1859), and Jean Yellin's authentication of Harriet Jacobs's
brilliant slave narrative, *Incidents in the Life of a Slave Girl*
(1861), a survey course spanning over a century and a quarter
emerged.

But the discovery of *Our Nig*, as well as the interest in
nineteenth-century black women's writing that this discovery
generated, convinced me that even the most curious and
diligent scholars knew very little of the extensive history
of the creative writings of Afro-American women before
1900. Indeed, most scholars of Afro-American literature
had never even read most of the books published by black
women, simply because these books—of poetry, novels, short
stories, essays, and autobiography—were mostly accessible only
in rare book sections of university libraries. For reasons un-
clear to me even today, few of these marvelous renderings of
the Afro-American woman's consciousness were reprinted in
the late 1960s and early 1970s, when so many other texts of
the Afro-American literary tradition were resurrected from
the dark and silent graveyard of the out-of-print and were
reissued in facsimile editions aimed at the hungry readership
for canonical texts in the nascent field of black studies.

So, with the help of several superb research assistants—
including David Curtis, Nicola Shilliam, Wendy Jones, Sam
Otter, Janadas Devan, Suvir Kaul, Cynthia Bond, Elizabeth
Alexander, and Adele Alexander—and with the expert advice

of scholars such as William Robinson, William Andrews, Mary Helen Washington, Maryemma Graham, Jean Yellin, Houston A. Baker, Jr., Richard Yarborough, Hazel Carby, Joan R. Sherman, Frances Foster, and William French, dozens of bibliographies were used to compile a list of books written or narrated by black women mostly before 1910. Without the assistance provided through this shared experience of scholarship, the scholar's true legacy, this project could not have been conceived. As the list grew, I was struck by how very many of these titles that I, for example, had never even heard of, let alone read, such as Ann Plato's *Essays*, Louisa Picquet's slave narrative, or Amelia Johnson's two novels, *Clarence and Corinne* and *The Hazeley Family*. Through our research with the Black Periodical Fiction and Poetry Project (funded by NEH and the Ford Foundation), I also realized that several novels by black women, including three works of fiction by Pauline Hopkins, had been serialized in black periodicals, but had never been collected and published as books. Nor had the several books of poetry published by black women, such as the prolific Frances E. W. Harper, been collected and edited. When I discovered still another "lost" novel by an Afro-American woman (*Four Girls at Cottage City*, published in 1898 by Emma Dunham Kelley-Hawkins), I decided to attempt to edit a collection of reprints of these works and to publish them as a "library" of black women's writings, in part so that I could read them myself.

Convincing university and trade publishers to undertake this project proved to be a difficult task. Despite the commercial success of *Our Nig* and of the several reprint series of women's works (such as Virago, the Beacon Black Women Writers Series, and Rutgers' American Women Writers Series), several presses rejected the project as "too large," "too limited," or as "commercially unviable." Only two publishers recognized the viability and the import of the project and, of these, Oxford's commitment to publish the titles simultaneously as a set made the press's offer irresistible.

While attempting to locate original copies of these exceedingly rare books, I discovered that most of the texts were housed at the Schomburg Center for Research in Black Culture, a branch of The New York Public Library, under the direction of Howard Dodson. Dodson's infectious enthusiasm for the project and his generous collaboration, as well as that of his stellar staff (especially Diana Lachatanere, Sharon Howard, Ellis Haizip, Richard Newman, and Betty Gubert), led to a joint publishing initiative that produced this set as part of the Schomburg's major fund-raising campaign. Without Dodson's foresight and generosity of spirit, the set would not have materialized. Without William P. Sisler's masterful editorship at Oxford and his staff's careful attention to detail, the set would have remained just another grand idea that tends to languish in a scholar's file cabinet.

I would also like to thank Dr. Michael Winston and Dr. Thomas C. Battle, Vice-President of Academic Affairs and the Director of the Moorland-Spingarn Research Center (respectively) at Howard University, for their unending encouragement, support, and collaboration in this project, and Esme E. Bhan at Howard for her meticulous research and bibliographical skills. In addition, I would like to acknowledge the aid of the staff at the libraries of Duke University, Cornell University (especially Tom Weissinger and Donald Eddy), the Boston Public Library, the Western Reserve Historical Society, the Library of Congress, and Yale University. Linda Robbins, Marion Osmun, Sarah Flanagan, and Gerard Case, all members of the staff at Oxford, were

extraordinarily effective at coordinating, editing, and producing the various segments of each text in the set. Candy
Ruck, Nina de Tar, and Phillis Molock expertly typed reams
of correspondence and manuscripts connected to the project.

I would also like to express my gratitude to my colleagues
who edited and introduced the individual titles in the set.
Without their attention to detail, their willingness to meet
strict deadlines, and their sheer enthusiasm for this project,
the set could not have been published. But finally and ulti-
mately, I would hope that the publication of the set would
help to generate even more scholarly interest in the black
women authors whose work is presented here. Struggling
against the seemingly insurmountable barriers of racism *and*
sexism, while often raising families and fulfilling full-time
professional obligations, these women managed nevertheless
to record their thoughts and feelings and to *testify* to all who
dare read them that the will to harness the power of collective
endurance and survival is the will to write.

The Schomburg Library of Nineteenth-Century Black
Women Writers is dedicated in memory of Pauline Augusta
Coleman Gates, who died in the spring of 1987. It was she
who inspired in me the love of learning and the love of literature. I have encountered in the books of this set no will
more determined, no courage more noble, no mind more
sublime, no self more celebratory of the achievements of all
Afro-American women, and indeed of life itself, than her
own.

A NOTE FROM
THE SCHOMBURG CENTER

Howard Dodson

The Schomburg Center for Research in Black Culture, The
New York Public Library, is pleased to join with Dr. Henry
Louis Gates and Oxford University Press in presenting The
Schomburg Library of Nineteenth-Century Black Women
Writers. This thirty-volume set includes the work of a generation of black women whose writing has only been available
previously in rare book collections. The materials reprinted
in twenty-four of the thirty volumes are drawn from the
unique holdings of the Schomburg Center.

A research unit of The New York Public Library, the
Schomburg Center has been in the forefront of those institutions dedicated to collecting, preserving, and providing
access to the records of the black past. In the course of its
two generations of acquisition and conservation activity, the
Center has amassed collections totaling more than 5 million
items. They include over 100,000 bound volumes, 85,000
reels and sets of microforms, 300 manuscript collections
containing some 3.5 million items, 300,000 photographs and
extensive holdings of prints, sound recordings, film and
videotape, newspapers, artworks, artifacts, and other book
and nonbook materials. Together they vividly document the
history and cultural heritages of people of African descent
worldwide.

Though established some sixty-two years ago, the Center's
book collections date from the sixteenth century. Its oldest
item, an Ethiopian Coptic Tunic, dates from the eighth or
ninth century. Rare materials, however, are most available

for the nineteenth-century African-American experience. It is from these holdings that the majority of the titles selected for inclusion in this set are drawn.

The nineteenth century was a formative period in African-American literary and cultural history. Prior to the Civil War, the majority of black Americans living in the United States were held in bondage. Law and practice forbade teaching them to read or write. Even after the war, many of the impediments to learning and literary productivity remained. Nevertheless, black men and women of the nineteenth century persevered in both areas. Moreover, more African-Americans than we yet realize turned their observations, feelings, social viewpoints, and creative impulses into published works. In time, this nineteenth-century printed record included poetry, short stories, histories, novels, autobiographies, social criticism, and theology, as well as economic and philosophical treatises. Unfortunately, much of this body of literature remained, until very recently, relatively inaccessible to twentieth-century scholars, teachers, creative artists, and others interested in black life. Prior to the late 1960s, most Americans (black as well as white) had never heard of these nineteenth-century authors, much less read their works.

The civil rights and black power movements created unprecedented interest in the thought, behavior, and achievements of black people. Publishers responded by revising traditional texts, introducing the American public to a new generation of African-American writers, publishing a variety of thematic anthologies, and reprinting a plethora of "classic texts" in African-American history, literature, and art. The reprints usually appeared as individual titles or in a series of bound volumes or microform formats.

The Schomburg Center, which has a long history of supporting publishing that deals with the history and culture of Africans in diaspora, became an active participant in many of the reprint revivals of the 1960s. Since hard copies of original printed works are the preferred formats for producing facsimile reproductions, publishers frequently turned to the Schomburg Center for copies of these original titles. In addition to providing such material, Schomburg Center staff members offered advice and consultation, wrote introductions, and occasionally entered into formal copublishing arrangements in some projects.

Most of the nineteenth-century titles reprinted during the 1960s, however, were by and about black men. A few black women were included in the longer series, but works by lesser known black women were generally overlooked. The Schomburg Library of Nineteenth-Century Black Women Writers is both a corrective to these previous omissions and an important contribution to Afro-American literary history in its own right. Through this collection of volumes, the thoughts, perspectives, and creative abilities of nineteenth-century African-American women, as captured in books and pamphlets published in large part before 1910, are again being made available to the general public. The Schomburg Center is pleased to be a part of this historic endeavor.

I would like to thank Professor Gates for initiating this project. Thanks are due both to him and Mr. William P. Sisler of Oxford University Press for giving the Schomburg Center an opportunity to play such a prominent role in the set. Thanks are also due to my colleagues at The New York Public Library and the Schomburg Center, especially Dr. Vartan Gregorian, Richard De Gennaro, Paul Fasana, Betsy

Pinover, Richard Newman, Diana Lachatanere, Glenderlyn Johnson, and Harold Anderson for their assistance and support. I can think of no better way of demonstrating than in this set the role the Schomburg Center plays in assuring that the black heritage will be available for future generations.

CONTENTS

This volume is dedicated to my parents,
who first sang and read to me our culture,
and to Margaret Walker
and J. Saunders Redding, mentors.

INTRODUCTION

Maryemma Graham

I belong to this race, and when it is down, I belong to a down race; when it is up, I belong to a risen race.[1]

This pronouncement was more than a public declaration for Frances Harper, whose literary importance is now being reassessed after nearly a century of silence. During her life Harper was regarded by her peers as a supremely oral poet, known for her professional activism in the cause of human rights for black people, women, and the poor. But for a woman who pioneered in the tradition of "protest" literature and whose immense popularity did a great deal to develop audiences for poetry in America, Harper's poetry has come to be seen as limited in craft, if not in vision. Her contribution to American letters has been viewed as worth noting, but only in passing. And when the Harper manuscripts and correspondence related to her publishing career were destroyed in the late 1950s, the writer seemed doomed to everlasting obscurity.[2]

Today this disparagement is discounted. The revival of interest in the life and work of Frances Ellen Watkins Harper has come about largely as a result of the efforts of feminist critics and historians, who have been attracted to her 1892 novel *Iola Leroy* and her active involvement in what has come to be called the "Woman's Era." This summation is provided by Barbara Christian:

That the first outpouring of Afro-American literature took
place within the context of a social movement was extremely
important for its development in the twentieth century. The
poet was seen as having a responsibility to her racial com-
munity, as well as to her own sensibility, and the discussion
of the condition of women was seen as an integral aspect of
black thought and expression rather than separate from it.[3]

Because Harper occupied a central position as a black
woman in a changing society more than a hundred years ago,
her poetry represents the continuity and progression of ideas
that brought together the major social movements of her era:
antislavery, women's suffrage, and temperance.

Born free in Baltimore in 1825 and orphaned at an early
age, Harper's interest in literature can be traced to her formal
education in a Baltimore school for free blacks founded and
run by her uncle. Most free blacks so educated were expected
to go into the teaching profession and were thus trained in
the classics, rhetoric, and the Bible. Harper was no exception.
And as was the custom for free, young, Northern black
women, she took a position as a live-in maid with a white
Baltimore family, the Armstrongs. There, her interest in
literature was stimulated. Mr. Armstrong owned a bookshop
and the fourteen-year-old Frances was a rather fortunate
nineteenth-century black domestic. Harper performed the
required household chores for the family and, since she could
read and write, was given access to the family library, and,
no doubt, spent considerable time in the bookshop. During
these years Harper developed more than an appreciation for
poetry, and about 1846, when she was in her early twenties,
her volume entitled *Forest Leaves* appeared. While employed
as the first female faculty member at Union Seminary,[4]
Harper became increasingly interested in the growing anti-

slavery movement. A move to Little York, Pennsylvania brought her closer to the antislavery cause and by 1854 Harper had moved into the Underground Railroad station in Philadelphia.[5] From 1854 until her death in 1911, Harper was totally devoted to her race and to the social causes in which she became engaged. Although she married Fenton Harper when she was thirty-five, she officially "retired" from public life for only a short while. After the birth of their daughter and Fenton Harper's death a few years later, Harper resumed her extremely active career.[6]

Harper calls to mind the person of Phillis Wheatley, who, though a slave, was taught to read and write and later would become a well-known poet. Like Wheatley and countless black female poets of succeeding generations, Harper would write popular poetry, enhanced by the fact that she was black and female, and would have her critical reputation suffer all the more because of it. But unlike Wheatley, whom she undoubtedly read, Harper was a committed artist and activist-intellectual, who openly embraced progressive and radical ideas in the nineteenth century in a profound challenge to American democracy.

Between 1854 and 1901, Harper wrote continuously while she was in the forefront of radical black and women's movements as a lecturer and public spokesperson. The resulting eleven books[7] of poetry and prose serve as a testament to this remarkable woman. Nevertheless, a critical biography has yet to appear, and the biographical data that does exist is embedded in William Still's nineteenth-century study of the Underground Railroad.[8]

Harper's life and work can be regarded as a model of ideological and political development and professional commitment. Maxwell Whiteman, for example, suggests that the modern concept of "black power" can be compared to Harper's ideas in numerous speeches and writings.[9] Feminist critics have suggested that Harper's convictions and the leadership role she played in a growing women's movement "inevitably led to feminist ideas."[10] Both suggestions are bound to open up an entirely new line of inquiry regarding Harper, one that will hopefully lead to more rigorous research to determine the extent to which she embraced positions in response to issues that troubled blacks and women in later decades.

Outside of her poetry and prose fiction, Harper was a major contributor to nineteenth-century documentary literature. Her writings appeared in almost every black independent publication of the period.[11] She wrote speeches and generally contributed original poetry for numerous occasional gatherings and was frequently quoted in the mainstream press. Because the bulk of this material remains uncollected, as are numerous letters she wrote to colleagues and friends, it is difficult to assess the full range and impact of Harper's ideas. It is an enormous task, of course, but one that begs for immediate and critical attention.

This edition of Harper's complete poems comes at an appropriate time in the reassessment of her canon. Its publication alone more than justifies the need to restore Harper to her proper social and literary context in the mid-nineteenth century and to see her development of the genre in which she wrote.

Harper's poetry canon is nevertheless difficult to reconstruct. It includes her self-published works, numerous printings of single editions, and a variety of expanded editions. It also includes variant poems appearing in nineteenth-century periodicals and other kinds of documentary literature, rigorous excursions into which have only recently become part of our scholarly enterprise.[12] Canon reconstruction is further complicated by the fact that information on Harper's frequent appearances at public gatherings, where she wrote and read one or more poems for the occasion, is extremely sparse.

Harper's poetry, while treating a wide range of themes on the general subjects of oppression, religion, and social and moral reform, falls into three major groups: those poems written in the years between 1854 and 1864, when she was a lecturer with the Maine Anti-Slavery Society; those written between 1865 and 1872, when Harper made at least two extensive tours of the South; and those written between 1872 and 1900, when she resided in Philadelphia and held leadership roles in a number of black, civil rights, and women's organizations and temperance societies.[13]

Harper's reputation largely rests on the circulation of some twenty editions of the volume *Poems on Miscellaneous Subjects*, published in 1854. These are nineteen decidedly public poems targeting the evils of slavery. Nearly half of the poems portray heroic slave men, women/mothers, and children. Separation is a dominant motif that permitted Harper to explore the abuses of slavery in a compelling manner. "The Slave Mother" is a good example of this antislavery sentiment in her early poetry.

> Saw you the sad, imploring eye?
>   Its every glance was pain,
> As if a storm of agony
>   Were sweeping through the brain.
>   . . . . . .
> He is not hers, although she bore
>   For him a mother's pains;
> He is not hers, although her blood
>   Is coursing through his veins!

The dramatic intensity builds in the poem as the narrative unfolds:

> They tear him from her circling arms,
>   Her last and fond embrace.
> Oh! never more may her sad eyes
>   Gaze on his mournful face.
>
> No marvel, then, these bitter shrieks
>   Disturb the listening air;
> She is a mother, and her heart
>   is breaking in despair.

Her frequent use of religious subjects and biblical imagery was consistent with the virtuous behavior that these poems extolled. Harper insists that one have "That Blessed Hope . . . amidst this world of strife (slavery)." One can see in this early volume a tendency to fuse Old Testament and New Testament ideologies,[14] a practice that would be consistent throughout her work. The contrast between the longed for "crown of life" from a kind, gentle Jesus, who promises peace, and "The mighty hand of God" who comes to redeem "Ethiopia" and free her people from their chains, illustrates the creative tension that provides internal unity for Harper's poetry. Within this religious and racial framework, Harper explores social, economic, and moral issues in "The Drunkard's Child" and "Report," where she warns: "Oh! wed not for beauty, / Though fair is the prize; / It may pall when you grasp it, / And fade in your eyes." Other such poems focus on poverty ("Died of Starvation"), love ("The Fugitive's Wife"), and death ("The Dying Christian" and "Eva's Farewell").

Poems on Miscellaneous Subjects serves as the model for *Poems* (1871), written during Harper's middle years. Al-

though this and subsequent volumes are not markedly different in the range of themes and ideas expressed, Harper's
travels through the South during Reconstruction and her own
personal situation altered the relationship of the poet to her
poetry. For one thing, chattel slavery was no longer an
immediate issue as she announced in the new era in "The
Freedom Bell." "Then ring, aye, ring the freedom bell, /
Proclaiming all the nation free; / Let earth with sweet thanksgiving swell / And heaven catch up the melody."

Second, Harper was subjected to bouts of bad health.
When she became ill, however, she continued to travel and
write. "Bury Me in a Free Land," written during one of her
periods of declining health, is an extremely telling example
of the fusion of emotions emerging from a personal situation
with those derived from an essentially social aesthetic. Here
is one of the few times that Harper personalizes the narrative
voice. She does not suppress or conceal her fear of her own
death, but is able to control the flow of emotions by drawing
a symbolic correlation with slavery as living death.

> I could not rest if around my grave
> I heard the steps of a trembling slave;
> His shadow above my silent tomb
> Would make it a place of fearful gloom.
>
> I could not rest if I heard the tread
> Of a coffle gang to the shambles led,
> And the mother's shriek of wild despair
> Rise like a curse on the trembling air.
> . . . . . .
> If I saw young girls from their mother's arms
> Bartered and sold for their youthful charms,
> My eye would flash with a mournful flame,
> My death-paled cheek grow red with shame.

I would sleep, dear friends, where bloated might
Can rob no man of his dearest right;
My rest shall be calm in any grave
Where none can call his brother a slave.

I ask no monument, proud and high
To arrest the gaze of the passers-by;
All that my yearning spirit craves,
Is bury me not in a land of slaves.

Aside from "Bury Me in a Free Land," there are a significant number of poems about death in this volume, the second of three collections published within a few years of Fenton
Harper's death. Witnessing the reality of the South for the
first time and coping with the death of a loved one as
well as her own illness, Harper moved the poems in this
volume away from explicitly racial subjects to more symbolic
ones. The poems about strength and sacrifice, love and truth,
work and regeneration all affirm Christian values.

The two other works emerging from the middle period
indicate the vitality of Harper's poetic imagination and something of the seriousness with which she took her craft. The
poems in these volumes are less imitative, and Harper appears
to be more comfortable with her subject matter, since she
pays more attention to structure and style. *Moses*, based on
the popular biblical story, one which Harper references in a
number of poems, is a long, allegorical work written in blank
verse. According to critic Melba Joyce Boyd, *Moses* is particularly significant first because it extends the popular biblical
story by incorporating the perspectives of two different women,
one Egyptian and one Hebrew, both mothers of Moses.
Second and more important, the poem has a profound cultural
significance. "[Moses] articulates in literary form the biblical
story that cultivates black Christianity during slavery. Har-

per's inclusion of Christ imagery inside the narrative of the Old Testament text clearly exemplified the intertwining of the two most critical biblical characters in black Christianity."[15] An examination of the biblical text and Harper's poem leads Boyd to conclude that "The dialogue is not taken from Exodus. . . . Harper infuses the woman's voice to qualify and extend the possibilities of the unseen and the unexplained."[16] *Moses* is unusual in that throughout the entire allegory Harper never refers to race, but narrates the story in such a way as to symbolize the hope and aspirations of black people. Harper could not avoid the moralizing tone of the long poem, written just after her return from an extended tour of the South. Lecturing and observing a newly freed black people, Harper used her influence and position to argue in support of civil rights for blacks and equal rights for women. Moses is presented as having a choice, and when he decides to return to help his people, he has rejected a pleasure-filled life for a life of sacrifice and commitment to a higher goal. The temperance themes are combined here with the prevailing Reconstruction ideology of social and moral uplift. *Moses* places Harper within a tradition where black religion, Afro-American cultural thought, and written discourse come together. It is in essence a radical tradition, one that supports a pronounced negation of selfhood and reinforces the nationality and liberation of black people.[17]

Sketches of Southern Life, Harper's last major volume of verse, shows a mature poet at her best. It is both a culmination of the formal structure Harper had used in her earliest poetry and an incorporation of a vernacular mode. The verse is infinitely lighter than *Moses*, and there is a characteristic ambiguity and irony in the lively narrative by Aunt Chloe, who recalls slavery, the Civil War, and emancipation (appropriately called "The Deliverance") and astutely sums up the current situation in the Reconstruction South. Harper expresses a broad array of social and cultural concerns in the text without being dependent on narrative intrusions. There is more focus on characterization than in any of her previous poems. Besides the principal narrator Aunt Chloe, there is Uncle Jacob, who represents the wisdom of his long years, a characteristic mysticism, and a significant degree of social consciousness. These narrators can be immediately distinguished from the typical slave narrators of the antebellum folk tale. Through Chloe's extended narration and four poems focusing on Reconstruction—"Aunt Chloe's Politics," "Learning to Read," "Church Building," and "The Reunion"—the reader is provided with a dynamic portrait of slave and rural life: the attitudes of slave masters at the advent of the Civil War; the selling of children and eventual reunion of families; the role of the church as the guardian of the social, spiritual, and moral life of black people; and the importance of literacy. In short, *Sketches of Southern Life* affirms and celebrates the institutional and cultural life of black people.

Moses and *Sketches of Southern Life* should be seen as complementary texts. For Harper, they represent an intellectual exploration into the meaning and nature of freedom. Taken together they form an important link in the evolution of the quest or journey motif in Afro-American autobiographical, poetic, and fictional discourse. By appropriating the Hebrew story of bondage and liberation, Harper looks back to the rhetorical devices and the mythology of the slave spirituals, to Harriet "Black Moses" Tubman, as well as to the spiritual autobiography and traditional slave narrative, where the narrator or autobiographer, according to William Andrews, proclaims "gospels of freedom."[18] *Moses* is a mod-

ified religious interpretation of the Afro-American quest for
freedom. The practice of exploring the historical experience
of black people through metaphor was not merely an extension
of a literary tradition but one which had tremendous significance in black thought and written expression in the rural
period.[19]

Moses was a prophet, leader, warrior, and a model of
revolutionary consciousness,[20] and his story lent itself to a
metaphorical treatment of the proverbial black leader. In
contrast, *Sketches* explores the meaning of freedom from the
perspective of the masses themselves. The shift from *Moses*
to *Sketches* is a shift from a focus on leadership to a focus on
the rank and file. Its characters are ex-slaves who have
journeyed from slavery to freedom, a journey to reclaim and
redefine their lives, their families, and their communities.

It is possible to make a case for reading these two texts as
an anticipation of some of the central themes and rhetorical
strategies appearing in Afro-American literature after Harper.[21] Aside from the appropriation of the biblical text, the
extension and elaboration of the journey motif is pervasive in
Afro-American writing. Dunbar's *Sport of the Gods* is at the
beginning of the tradition in modern black literature, which
novelizes the slave narrative tradition and makes a place for
it in the discourse of urban black writers.[22]

Structurally, a similar pattern of development can be seen
in Harper's poetry. The vast majority of her poems used
conventional metrical patterns, ranging from the rhymed
couplet to the four-line ballad stanza, a popular narrative
form with end-rhyme occurring alternately in an "abcb"
pattern or in sequence as an "aabb" pattern. The third person
narrative framework accommodated Harper's descriptive and
performance-oriented style. For the modern reader these

poems seem imitative and forced, wedded to a metrical system
and style that too often sacrificed depth of thought, subtlety
of imagery, and precision of language for melodrama and
didacticism. Ironically, among this body of poetry—which
has been described as pedestrian, mechanical, lacking concreteness and control—are those poems for which Harper is
best remembered, including "The Slave Auction," "The
Present Age," "A Double Standard," and her most anthol-
ogized, "Bury Me in a Free Land." Harper's heavy reliance
on oral delivery was the *modus operandi* for her poetry.
Lacking methods for investigating oral performance poetry
places us at a loss in exploring this line of analysis.

   Moses: A Story of the Nile, first published in 1869 and
enlarged as *Idylls of the Bible* in 1901, varies from the ballad
metrical pattern in a forty-page biblical allegory in blank
verse. Here Harper varies line length and uses other lin-
guistic devices to better convey the imagery and rich symbolic
content of the story. A third type of poetry is perhaps Harper's
most important literary contribution. *Sketches of Southern Life*
is a series of connected narratives in the first person. The
black vernacular voice is neither exaggerated nor highly
stylized, substituting the more popular folk tale dialect pop-
ularized by Charles Chesnutt and Joel Chandler Harris.
According to Boyd, Harper shows her mastery of technique
by adjusting the ballad structure to convey the rhythmical
nuances of black oral discourse. Thus, Harper deserves more
careful study as a transcriber of Afro-American dialect into
literature.[23]

   During the period between 1872 and 1900, although her
interest shifted somewhat from poetry to fiction, there were
at least forty additional poems that appeared for the first
time.[24] The dates of the three small volumes containing most

of these poems have not been confirmed, but in 1895, three years after the publication of *Iola Leroy*, the poems comprising these volumes were apparently all included in *Atlanta Offering: Poems*. The influence of her temperance work is apparent in poems such as "The Pure in Heart Shall See God," and "The Burdens of All," but these poems permit a multiplicity of possible interpretations. They register a strong statement by a woman who sees her life's work as nearly done. Couched in religious metaphor, the description of her life's work is nevertheless clear. She has answered the charge: "Go work in my vineyard, said the Lord, / and gather the bruised grain; / . . . Though thorns may often pierce my feet, / And the shadows still abide, / The mists will vanish before His smile, / There will be light at eventide." In "Renewal of Strength," Harper speaks quite openly, accepting the inevitable gracefully: "For me a dimness slowly creeps / Around earth's fairest light, / But heaven grows clearer to my view, / And fairer to my sight."

It is interesting to note that critics often found it difficult to comment on Harper's literary achievement in those works that gained immense popularity, namely, *Poems on Miscellaneous Subjects* and *Sketches of Southern Life*. Only when referring to her nonracial verse is there some indication that Harper's achievements were worthy of distinction. Vernon Loggins, for example, preferred not to take *Moses* as a racial allegory and complimented Harper's achievement in a work that had "nothing to say about the Negro." [25] More frequently critics have accepted Harper's historical significance, but have had difficulty with the aggressive link she made between poetry and politics. Early biographers [26] focused their attention on Harper's antislavery activity while early literary critics practically dismissed her novel and called her poetry "banal

and trite."[27] Social histories and contemporary literary criticism reclaim Harper, but the focus has shifted more to a
consideration of the feminist preoccupations in her speeches
and political rhetoric and the discursive practices suggested
by *Iola Leroy*.

In this proliferation of current scholarship, her poetry has
continued to receive little attention. It has not replaced, for
example, the early work of J. Saunders Redding who con-
siders Harper's canon from an aesthetic and sociohistorical
perspective.[28] French scholar Jean Wagner, who undertook
a study of black poetry from Dunbar to Hughes, comments
on Harper only in passing, concluding that there was no
"true black poet before Dunbar."[29] And Theodora Daniel's
unpublished thesis remains the only comprehensive overview
and compilation of Harper's creative work to date.

The difficulty that is presented to the reader or critic who
wishes to know Harper is that which is common to any study
of black women writers in the nineteenth century: In what
tradition should the writer be placed? Harper belongs not to
one, but to three traditions—genteel, black liberation, and
prefeminist. Likewise, her commitment to the achievement
of human rights in the nineteenth century brings into play
the multiple dimensions of race and nationality, class and
gender.

Harper had a clear vision of the rich and fertile heritage
of black people. As a black poet, she found a continuous need
to make this heritage manifest. The "Dying Bondman"
illustrates this:

> He had been an Afric chieftain,
> Worn his manhood as a crown;
> But upon the field of battle
> Had been fiercely stricken down.

The bondman is exalted as he struggles to maintain his historical dignity:

> "Master," said the dying bondman,
> "Home and friends I soon shall see;
> But before I reach my country,
> Master write that I am free;
>
> "For the spirits of my fathers
> Would shrink back from me in pride,
> If I told them at our greeting
> I a slave had lived and died;—"

This type of racial consciousness takes on other manifestations which are, in fact, more representative of the nationality of black people and the affirmation and expression of group identity.[30] It can be seen as the need to define oneself in opposition to individual and group oppression and to engage in culture-defining activities. Harper's use of black speech, the attention given to the role of black institutions, and the importance placed on the achievement of literacy—as a way of defining oneself in relation to one's own experience—are all examples of an expressed nationality of black people in late nineteenth-century America. This concept is most explicit in *Sketches of Southern Life* and the characterization of Aunt Chloe. She becomes the metaphor for black liberation, the link between the expressed ideal of freedom and the reality of its achievement.

If Harper understood what it meant to be black in nineteenth-century America, she was particularly concerned, as recent criticism has suggested, about the impact of slavery and racism on women. For Harper, there could be no fate worse than the moral and human degradation experienced by black women. All aspects of a woman's life are described. Although the portrait of a slave mother torn away from her child was a moving and sentimental subject for appeal, the number of poems on the subject of women also suggests the complexity of the black woman's relationship to slavery: supporting her son who becomes a martyr for freedom, sending a fugitive husband to death in order to save the family, escaping to freedom alone with her children, having both her body and her labor exploited because she was black, a woman, and a slave.

The dramatic intensity of "Eliza Harris" and "To the Union Savers of Cleveland" is characteristic of Harper's ability to capture the slave experience through her portraits of women. Her didacticism in poems such as "Advice to the Girls," "Report," and "A Double Standard" reflects a genuine sensitivity to gender-based issues long before they would become apparent in the poetic discourse of women writers. "Vashti" is a courageous queen who will not submit to personal degradation by the King.

> "Go, tell the King," she proudly said,
>   "That I am Persia's Queen,
> And by his crowds of merry men
>   I never will be seen.
>
> "I'll take the crown from off my head
>   And tread it 'neath my feet,
> Before their rude and careless gaze
>   My shrinking eyes shall meet."

She thus becomes a martyr to "womanhood" when the King takes away her crown:

> She heard again the King's command,
>   And left her high estate;
> Strong in her earnest womanhood,
>   She calmly met her fate.

> And left the palace of the King,
> Proud of her spotless name—
> A woman who could bend to grief,
> But would not bow to shame.

In *Sketches of Southern Life*, Harper's most extensive use of the female voice, Chloe's controlling vision sets the temporal logic of the narrative. The first person narrative is related in six sections, beginning with Chloe's children being sold into slavery and ending when they are all united for the first time. Chloe thus interweaves her personal story with the flow of Afro-American history.

The thematic focus on women and gender-related issues has its source in Harper's political activism, which itself took on several manifestations—political reform, civil rights, and Christian humanism. To ignore or minimize the racial and class content of this activism, however, is to underestimate the degree of Harper's understanding of the social and economic structure of society. In a letter to William Still, Harper reveals the depth of her understanding:

> Now . . . I hold that between the white people and the colored there is a community of interests . . . but that community of interests does not consist in increasing the privileges of one class and curtailing the rights of the other, but in getting every citizen interested in the welfare, progress and durability of the state.[31]

Seldom overtly political in her poetry, Harper nevertheless could be moved beyond her generally composed and temperate nature. In "An Appeal to My Country Women," she is visibly disturbed. Structured as a statement/response, the poem is a good illustration of the intersection of race, class, and gender. The poet almost seems to be holding back her indignation. "You can sigh o'er the sad-eyed Armenian / . . .

You can sorrow o'er little children / . . . For beasts you have gentle compassion." The response bursts forth abruptly:

> But hark! from our Southland are floating
>   Sobs of anguish, murmurs of pain,
> And women heart-stricken are weeping
>   Over their tortured and their slain.
>   . . . . . .
>
> When we plead for the wrecked and fallen,
>   The exile from far-distant shores,
> Remember that men are still wasting
>   Life's crimson around our own doors.
>
> Have ye not, oh, my favored sisters,
>   Just a plea, a prayer or a tear,
> For mothers who dwell 'neath the shadows
>   Of agony, hatred and fear?

The mix of aesthetic modes in Harper's poetry shows a variety of influences. Afro-American folk expression in nine-teenth-century America produced a large oral lore, composed of sacred and secular traditions. All of these expressions bore a strong, dramatic, and vivid sense of the present, even in their projection of a different world, a sense that Harper replicates in her poetry. This strong sense of orality carried over into Afro-American formal literature and represents a tradition that joins together what critic William Robinson calls "orator poets," for example, Lucy Terry, Jupiter Ham-mon, George Moses Horton, James Whitfield, and James Madison Bell.[32] While Harper's work appears to be a con-solidation of this tradition in Afro-American writing, it is distinctive in the author's preference for the concrete rather than the abstract and metaphysical.

This concreteness has as much to do with Harper's literary style as it does her social vision. In "Songs for the People," Harper makes her aesthetic preferences known.

Let me make the songs for the people,
　　Songs for the old and young;
Songs to stir like a battle-cry
　　Wherever they are sung.
　　　　· · · · · ·

Let me make the songs for the weary,
　　Amid life's fever and fret,
Till hearts shall relax their tension,
　　And careworn brows forget.
　　　　· · · · · ·

I would sing for the poor and aged,
　　When shadows dim their sight;
Of the bright and restful mansions,
　　Where there shall be no night.

Our world, so worn and weary,
　　Needs music, pure and strong,
To hush the jangle and discords
　　Of sorrow, pain, and wrong.

These celebratory lines not only foreshadow Margaret
Walker's literary masterpiece "For My People," but also
anticipate the urban militancy of Don L. Lee/Haki Madhu-
buti, Sonia Sanchez, and LeRoi Jones/Amiri Baraka.[33] Like
these black people in succeeding generations, Harper found
little use for a romantic celebration of the past, but concerned
herself instead with the day-to-day reality of nineteenth-
century American slavery and its aftermath.

Nineteenth-century writers of sentimental poetry in the
genteel tradition—specifically, the Fireside poets: Lowell,
Whittier, Longfellow, Holmes, and Bryant—were also part
of Harper's poetic nourishment. She was particularly attracted
to Whittier's poems of social reform and Longfellow's dramatic narratives, which provided her with models for many
of the poems in her two most popular collections, *Poems on*

Miscellaneous Subjects and *Sketches of Southern Life*. Whittier and Longfellow, along with the intellectual climate of the period, offered her a deep sense of moral piety that carried through to the religious poems comprising her later volumes.

An overall assessment of Frances Harper and her relationship to Afro-American literature and black women's literature is a task not easily accomplished. Her location in the configuration of American and even world literary traditions is even more problematic. She was not a formalist but showed a consciousness of the literary techniques common in the poetry of her era. Her ability to use a variety of narrative styles and to experiment with language was consistent in her poetry and in her prose. Harper's real significance in terms of form, however, lies in the extent to which she consolidated the oral tradition and the ballad form. The rhymed quatrain was used by poets writing in the sentimental tradition. But Harper's addition of dramatic details, vivid imagery, and her effective understanding of Afro-American life, together with her political sensibility, transformed the common ballad into a distinctly Afro-American discourse.

If the phrase "social protest poetry" was coined as a result of Harper's popular work, it was made all the more powerful because of her awareness of race and nationality, class, and gender issues that were at the core of her poetry.

Even with this volume of Harper's published poetry and the reissue of *Iola Leroy*[34] the canon is far from complete, and it is certainly too soon to consider a definitive assessment. In any case, Harper stands at a critical juncture in the development of Afro-American poetry. By merging elements of the folk and the formal, and oral and written forms of discourse, she prefigured the work of Paul Laurence Dunbar,

Charles Chesnutt, Langston Hughes, Sterling Brown, and Margaret Walker, as well as an entire generation of Black Arts Movement poets in the 1960s. It is this tradition—and Harper is its pioneering voice—that renounces "art for art's sake." Frances Harper's poetry is the intellectual endowment of an entire age; her life, a shared social vision imparted to us all.

NOTES

1. Frances Ellen Watkins Harper quoted in William Still, *The Underground Railroad*, (Philadelphia: Porter and Coates, 1872) p. 773.

2. In the "Introduction" to *Poems on Miscellaneous Subjects*, reprinted by Rhistoric Publications (Philadelphia) in 1969, Maxwell Whiteman offers the following commentary: "Merrihew and Thompson, the antislavery publishers of Philadelphia, issued many of [Harper's] books. When that company retired from business, the stereotype plates were sold to the firm of Ferguson and Company. In the late 1950s Ferguson sold out their business, and some of Mrs. Harper's remaining stock, manuscripts, and correspondence were discarded as rubbish."

3. Barbara Christian, *Black Feminist Criticism* (Elmsford, NY: Pergamon Press, 1985), p. 121.

4. Located near Columbus, Ohio, Union was a school for free blacks founded in 1847 by the African Methodist Episcopal Church.

5. A major influence on Harper's decision to give up her teaching career and join the antislavery cause was abolitionist William Still, widely known for his work on the Underground Railroad, who was to remain one of Harper's closest friends throughout her lifetime.

6. For a more detailed summary of Harper's life and work, see Maryemma Graham, "The Threefold Cord: Blackness, Womanness

and Art, A Study of the Life and Work of Frances Ellen Watkins Harper," Master's Thesis, Cornell University, 1973.

7. There are six known expanded editions of the published poetry not included in this count.

8. Still reconstructs a biography of Harper from his own information and the extensive correspondence between them.

9. Whiteman comments as follows: "Mrs. Harper wrote in a burst of confidence: 'We have the brain power, we have the muscle power, and in all the rebel states we have political power.'" In doing so she defined the essential positive ingredients of black power. "Introduction," to *Poems on Miscellaneous Subjects by Frances Ellen Watkins*, n.p.

10. See Paula Giddings' *When and Where I Enter: The Impact of Black Women on Race and Sex in America* (New York: Morrow, 1984) for a discussion of Harper's role in nineteenth-century feminist thought; Bert James Loewenberg and Ruth Bogin's *Black Women in Nineteenth-Century American Life: Their Words, Their Thoughts, Their Feelings*, (University Park: Pennsylvania State University Press, 1976) for selected speeches and essays by Harper; and Hazel V. Carby's "Introduction" to the Beacon edition of *Iola Leroy, or Shadows Uplifted* (Boston: Beacon Press, 1987), Barbara Christian's *Black Feminist Criticism*, and Erlene Stetson's *Black Sister: Poetry by Black American Women, 1746–1980* (Bloomington: Indiana University Press, 1981) for textual interpretations of Harper's feminism.

11. See Theodora Williams Daniel, "The Poems of Frances E. W. Harper, Edited with a Biographical and Critical Introduction and Bibliography," Master's Thesis, Howard University, 1937. Daniel provides a bibliography of publications in which Harper's work appeared.

12. For example, the Afro-American Novel Project at the University of Mississippi has a database of over 1,100 Afro-American novels published since 1853; the Black Periodical Fiction and Poetry Project, begun at Yale and now located at Cornell University, has uncovered 12,500 works of fiction, 28,200 poems, and 45,000 book

reviews and literary notices to date; the American Fiction Project at Ohio State University, with a database of American fiction between 1901 and 1925, has identified 6,000 titles; and the Black Abolitionist Papers Project at Florida State University is working specifically on materials published by black antislavery activists.

13. Harper fought against the racist practices in a number of organizations. At the same time she consistently upheld the policies of such organizations. For details see Giddings, *When and Where I Enter*, pp. 71–73.

14. Joan R. Sherman has a brief but insightful discussion of this in her chapter devoted to Harper in *Invisible Poets: Afro-Americans of the Nineteenth Century* (Urbana: University of Illinois Press, 1979), pp. 67–69.

15. This manuscript, *Discarded Legacy: A Critical Study of Frances Ellen Watkins Harper* by Melba Joyce Boyd (forthcoming from the University of Mississippi Press), provides the most extensive critical treatment of Harper's poetry and fiction, p. 7.

16. Boyd, p. 24.

17. The most extensive discussion of a revolutionary tradition in Afro-American literature has been given by Amiri Baraka (LeRoi Jones). See *Dagger and Javelins: Essays* (New York: Quill, 1984), especially the essays "The Revolutionary Tradition in Afro-American Literature," pp. 137–48, and "Afro-American Literature and Class Struggle," pp. 310–34.

18. William Andrews, *To Tell a Free Story: The First Century of Afro-American Autobiography 1760–1865* (Urbana: University of Illinois Press, 1986), p. 17.

19. The talented tenth philosophy was espoused by W. E. B. Du Bois and others, including Harper. The issue of black leadership was viewed in connection with this philosophy.

20. Boyd, p. 41.

21. Boyd argues that a Moses or "Mosaic" motif is persistent in Afro-American poetry, citing the works of Paul Laurence Dunbar ("Ante-bellum Sermon"), Langston Hughes ("I've Known Rivers"), Jean Toomer *(Cane)*, Robert Hayden ("Runnegate, Runnegate"),

and Margaret Walker *(Prophets for a New Day)*, as well as in the fiction of Zora Neale Hurston *(Moses, Man of the Mountain)*.

22. Examples of this include Booker T. Washington's *Up From Slavery*, James Weldon Johnson's *The Autobiography of an Ex-Colored Man*, Zora Neale Hurston's *Their Eyes Were Watching God*, Richard Wright's *Black Boy*, Ralph Ellison's *Invisible Man*, Ernest Gaines' *The Autobiography of Miss Jane Pittman*, Amiri Baraka's *System of Dante's Hell*, Toni Morrison's *Song of Solomon*, and most of the works by contemporary black women writers who also explore this journey motif in a symbolic and thematic manner.

23. Boyd, p. 8. There are several discussions of Afro-American dialect transcription. See, for example, the analysis of this problem in Charles T. Davis and Henry Louis Gates, Jr., eds., *The Slave's Narrative* (New York: Oxford University Press, 1985).

24. *Iola Leroy, or Shadows Uplifted* (Philadelphia: Garrigues Brothers, 1892) is Harper's major work of fiction.

25. Vernon Loggins, *The Negro Author: His Development in America* (New York: Columbia University Press, 1931), p. 343.

26. See William Still, *Underground Railroad*, pp. 755–80; Lawson Scruggs, *Women of Distinction* (Raleigh, NC: by the author, 1893); Samuel Sillen, *Women Against Slavery* (New York: Masses & Mainstream, 1955); George Bragg, *Men of Maryland* (Baltimore: Church Advocate Press, 1925); and Hallie Brown, *Homespun Heroines and Other Women of Distinction* (Xenia, OH: The Aldine Publishing Company, 1926).

27. Sterling Brown, *Negro Poetry and Drama and The Negro in American Fiction* (New York: Atheneum, 1969), p. 11.

28. J. Saunders Redding, *To Make a Poet Black* (Chapel Hill: University of North Carolina Press, 1939), see pages 38–44.

29. Jean Wagner, *Black Poets of the United States: From Paul Laurence Dunbar to Langston Hughes*, trans. Kenneth Douglass (Urbana: University of Illinois Press, 1973), p. 22.

30. For a fuller discussion see Abdul Alkalimat and Associates, *Introduction to Afro-American Studies: A Peoples College Primer* (Chicago: Twenty-First Century Books, 1986), pp. 24; 81–96; 172–

75. The terms race, class, nationality, and ideology, when combined with seven stages of historical development, are the units of analysis in a paradigmatic framework suggested in this text for examining the Afro-American experience.

31. Still, *Underground Railroad*, p. 770.

32. William Robinson, ed., *Early Black American Poets* (Dubuque, IA: M.C. Brown Company, 1969), pp. 3–83.

33. See Eugene Redmond, *Drumvoices: The Mission of Afro-American Poetry* (Garden City, NJ: Anchor Press, 1976).

34. Beacon, 1987; Oxford University Press, 1988.

EDITORIAL NOTE

The poems that appear here include the one hundred sixteen poems in ten separate volumes of Harper's poetry issued between 1854 and 1901. Ten additional poems are from other sources, most of which were identified by Theodora Williams Daniel. Four volumes produced the majority of the poems: *Poems on Miscellaneous Subjects* (1854), *Moses: A Story of the Nile* (1869), *Poems* (1871), and *Sketches of Southern Life* (1872). The smaller volumes *The Sparrow's Fall* (n.d.) and, with the exception of two poems, *The Martyr of Alabama* (ca. 1894), are all included in the 1895 volume, *Atlanta Offering: Poems*. Expanded editions of previously published volumes were the sources for a number of poems: an 1857 edition of *Poems on Miscellaneous Subjects*; *Moses*, with new poems appearing in 1889 and even more new ones in 1893; an 1888 edition of *Sketches of Southern Life*; and *Atlanta Offering: Poems*, published under the title *Poems*, with additional poems appearing in 1898 and 1900.

As indicated above, an exact publishing history for the extant volumes is confusing and difficult to document. The work of Theodora W. Daniel has not been superseded in this regard, an assessment which can be made of many early graduate theses produced at historically black institutions. Daniel was able to complete a comprehensive bibliography of Harper's poetry, fiction, and prose writings that were still in circulation in 1937. Although her critical discussion of the poetry is somewhat limited, she provides useful annotations for the poetry books and booklets, points out the discrepancies

between cover pages and title pages, and documents certain
inconsistencies in the indexing procedure that are important
clues for any scholar dealing with nineteenth-century published material.* Daniel's particular contribution, however,
was her careful examination of the extant volumes, noting the
additional poems that appeared in new and expanded editions
and documenting variant readings. In addition to the poems
identified in Daniel's archival research, one poem was discovered by another scholar doing unrelated research, suggesting
the direction that future research on Harper might take.†
We have followed Mrs. Daniel's lead by providing an index
to Harper's poetry volumes according to the date of their
original publication, the contents of each extant volume, and
the Harper poetry holdings at the three major research
collections. This should prove useful to any scholar or interested reader who might want to do further study on Harper.

---

*Some discrepancies had been initially identified and cited in the *Catalog of
the Arthur B. Spingarn Collection of Negro Authors*, Howard University,
Washington, D.C. I am extremely grateful to Betty M. Culpepper of the
Moorland-Spingarn Collection for bringing to my attention some of the
difficulties in reconstructing the publishing history of the Harper manuscripts, the most complete collection of which are housed in Howard
University's rare books room.

†Leslie J. Pollard reported on two poems by Harper in "Frances Harper
and the Old People: Two Recently Discovered Poems," *The Griot* 4 (Sum-
mer/Winter 1985): 52–56. The poems were published in an annual report
of the Philadelphia Home for the Aged and Infirm Colored Persons, a
source for the author's dissertation on the home's history. Only one of the
two poems had not previously appeared in Harper's published collections.

Complete Poems of
Frances E. W. Harper

THE SYROPHENICIAN WOMAN

Joy to my bosom! rest to my fear!
Judea's prophet draweth near!
Joy to my bosom! peace to my heart!
Sickness and sorrow before him depart!

Rack'd with agony and pain,
Writhing, long my child has lain;
Now the prophet draweth near,
All our griefs shall disappear.

"Lord!" she cried with mournful breath,
"Save! Oh, save my child from death!"
But as though she was unheard,
Jesus answered not a word.

With a purpose naught could move,
And the seal of woman's love,
Down she knelt in anguish wild—
"Master! save, Oh! save my child!"

" 'Tis not meet," the Savior said,
"Thus to waste the children's bread;
I am only sent to seek
Israel's lost and scattered sheep."

"True," she said, "Oh, gracious Lord,
True and faithful is thy word:
But the humblest, meanest, may
Eat the crumbs they cast away."

"Woman," said th' astonish'd Lord,
"Be it even as thy word!
By thy faith that knows no fail,
Thou hast ask'd, and shalt prevail."

3

THE SLAVE MOTHER

Heard you that shriek? It rose
   So wildly on the air,
It seemed as if a burden'd heart
   Was breaking in despair.

Saw you those hands so sadly clasped—
   The bowed and feeble hand—
The shuddering of that fragile form—
   That look of grief and dread?

Saw you the sad, imploring eye?
   Its every glance was pain,
As if a storm of agony
   Were sweeping through the brain.

She is a mother, pale with fear,
   Her boy clings to her side,
And in her kirtle vainly tries
   His trembling form to hide.

He is not hers, although she bore
   For him a mother's pains;
He is not hers, although her blood
   Is coursing through his veins!

He is not hers, for cruel hands
   May rudely tear apart
The only wreath of household love
   That binds her breaking heart.

His love has been a joyous light
   That o'er her pathway smiled,
A fountain gushing ever new,
   Amid life's desert wild.

His lightest word has been a tone
   Of music round her heart,

Their lives a streamlet blent in one—
    Oh, Father! must they part?

They tear him from her circling arms,
    Her last and fond embrace.
Oh! never more may her sad eyes
    Gaze on his mournful face.

No marvel, then, these bitter shrieks
    Disturb the listening air;
She is a mother, and her heart
    Is breaking in despair.

BIBLE DEFENCE OF SLAVERY

Take sackcloth of the darkest dye,
    And shroud the pulpits round!
Servants of Him that cannot lie,
    Sit mourning on the ground.

Let holy horror blanch each cheek,
    Pale every brow with fears:
And rocks and stones, if ye could speak,
    Ye well might melt to tears!

Let sorrow breathe in every tone,
    In every strain ye raise;
Insult not God's majestic throne
    With th' mockery of praise.

A reverend man, whose light should be
    The guide of age and youth,
Brings to the shrine of slavery
    The sacrifice of truth!

For the direst wrong of man imposed,
    Since Sodom's fearful cry,

The word of life has been enclosed,
   To give your God the lie.

Oh! when we pray for the heathen lands,
   And plead for their dark shores,
Remember Slavery's cruel hands
   Make heathens at your doors!

ELIZA HARRIS

Like a fawn from the arrow, startled and wild,
A woman swept by us, bearing a child;
In her eyes was the night of a settled despair,
And her brow was o'ershaded with anguish and care.

She was nearing the river—in reaching the brink,
She heeded no danger, she paused not to think;
For she is a mother—her child is a slave—
And she'll give him his freedom, or find him a grave!

It was a vision to haunt us, that innocent face—
So pale in its aspect, so fair in its grace;
As the tramp of the horse and the bay of the hound,
With the fetters that gall, were trailing the ground!

She was nerv'd by despair, and strengthened by woe,
As she leap'd o'er the chasms that yawn'd from below;
Death howl'd in the tempest, and rav'd in the blast,
But she heard not the sound till the danger was past.

Oh! how shall I speak of my proud country's shame
Of the stains on her glory, how give them their name?
How say that her banner in mockery waves—
Her star-spangled banner—o'er millions of slaves?

How say that the lawless may torture and chase
A woman whose crime is the hue of her face?
How the depths of the forest may echo around
With the shrieks of despair, and the bay of the hound?

With her step on the ice, and her arm on her child,
The danger was fearful, the pathway was wild;
But, aided by Heaven, she gained a free shore,
Where the friends of humanity open'd their door.

So fragile and lovely, so fearfully pale,
Like a lily that bends to the breath of the gale,
Save the heave of her breast, and the sway of her hair,
You'd have thought her a statue of fear and despair.

In agony close to her bosom she press'd
The life of her heart, the child of her breast—
Oh! love from its tenderness gathering might,
Had strengthen'd her soul for the dangers of light.

But she's free:—yes, free from the land where the slave
From the hound of oppression must rest in the grave;
Where bondage and torture, where scourges and drains
Have plac'd on our banner indelible stains.

The bloodhounds have miss'd the scent of her way;
The hunter is rifled and foil'd of his prey;
Fierce jargon and cursing, with clanking of chains,
Make sounds of strange discord on Liberty's plains.

With the rapture of love and fulness of bliss,
She plac'd on his brow a mother's fond kiss:—
Oh! poverty, danger and death she can brave,
For the child of her love is no longer a slave!

ETHIOPIA

Yes! Ethiopia yet shall stretch
    Her bleeding hands abroad;
Her cry of agony shall reach
    The burning throne of God.

The tyrant's yoke from off her neck,
    His fetters from her soul,
The mighty hand of God shall break,
    And spurn the base control.

Redeemed from dust and freed from chains,
    Her sons shall lift their eyes;
From cloud-capt hills and verdant plains
    Shall shouts of triumph rise.

Upon her dark, despairing brow,
    Shall play a smile of peace;
For God shall bend unto her wo,
    And bid her sorrows cease.

'Neath sheltering vines and stately palms
    Shall laughing children play,
And aged sires with joyous psalms
    Shall gladden every day.

Secure by night, and blest by day,
    Shall pass her happy hours;
Nor human tigers hunt for prey
    Within her peaceful bowers.

Then, Ethiopia! stretch, oh! stretch
    Thy bleeding hands abroad;
Thy cry of agony shall reach
    And find redress from God.

THE DRUNKARD'S CHILD

He stood beside his dying child,
    With a dim and bloodshot eye;
They'd won him from the haunts of vice
    To see his first-born die.

He came with a slow and staggering tread,
    A vague, unmeaning stare,
And, reeling, clasped the clammy hand,
    So deathly pale and fair.

In a dark and gloomy chamber,
    Life ebbing fast away,
On a coarse and wretched pallet,
    The dying sufferer lay:
A smile of recognition
    Lit up the glazing eye;
"I'm very glad," it seemed to say,
    "You've come to see me die."

That smile reached to his callous heart,
    It sealed fountains stirred;
He tried to speak, but on his lips
    Faltered and died each word.
And burning tears like rain
    Poured down his bloated face,
Where guilt, remorse and shame
    Had scathed, and left their trace.

"My father!" said the dying child,
    (His voice was faint and low,)
"Oh! clasp me closely to your heart,
    And kiss me ere I go.
Bright angels beckon me away,
    To the holy city fair—
Oh! tell me, Father, ere I go,
    Say, will you meet me there?"

He clasped him to his throbbing heart,
    "I will! I will!" he said;
His pleading ceased—the father held
    His first-born and his dead!

The marble brow, with golden curls,
  Lay lifeless on his breast;
Like sunbeams on the distant clouds
  Which line the gorgeous west.

THE SLAVE AUCTION

The sale began—young girls were there,
  Defenceless in their wretchedness,
Whose stifled sobs of deep despair
  Revealed their anguish and distress.

And mothers stood with streaming eyes,
  And saw their dearest children sold;
Unheeded rose their bitter cries,
  While tyrants bartered them for gold.

And woman, with her love and truth—
  For these in sable forms may dwell—
Gaz'd on the husband of her youth,
  With anguish none may paint or tell.

And men, whose sole crime was their hue,
  The impress of their Maker's hand,
And frail and shrinking children, too,
  Were gathered in that mournful band.

Ye who have laid your love to rest,
  And wept above their lifeless clay,
Know not the anguish of that breast,
  Whose lov'd are rudely torn away.

Ye may not know how desolate
  Are bosoms rudely forced to part,
And how a dull and heavy weight
  Will press the life-drops from the heart.

THE REVEL

"He knoweth not that the dead are there."

In yonder halls reclining
   Are forms surpassing fair,
And brilliant lights are shining,
   But, oh! the dead are there!

There's music, song and dance,
   There's banishment of care,
And mirth in every glance,
   But, oh! the dead are there!

The wine cup's sparkling glow
   Blends with the viands rare,
There's revelry and show,
   But still, the dead are there!

'Neath that flow of song and mirth
   Runs the current of despair,
But the simple sons of earth
   Know not the dead are there!

They'll shudder start and tremble,
   They'll weep in wild despair
When the solemn truth breaks on them,
   That the dead, the dead are there!

THAT BLESSED HOPE

Oh! crush it not, that hope so blest,
   Which cheers the fainting heart,
And points it to the coming rest,
   Where sorrow has no part.

Tear from my heart each worldly prop,
    Unbind each earthly string,
But to this blest and glorious hope,
    Oh! let my spirit cling.

It cheer'd amid the days of old
    Each holy patriarch's breast;
It was an anchor to their souls,
    Upon it let me rest.

When wandering in dens and caves,
    In sheep and goat skins dress'd,
A peel'd and scatter'd people learned
    To know this hope was blest.

Help me, amidst this world of strife,
    To long for Christ to reign,
That when He brings the crown of life,
    I may that crown obtain!

THE DYING CHRISTIAN

The light was faintly streaming
    Within a darkened room,
Where a woman, faint and feeble,
    Was sinking to the tomb.

The silver cord was loosened,
    We knew that she must die;
We read the mournful token
    In the dimness of her eye.

We read it in the radiance
    That lit her pallid cheek,
And the quivering of the feeble lip,
    Too faint its joys to speak.

Like a child oppressed with slumber,
　　She calmly sank to rest,
With her trust in her Redeemer,
　　And her heart upon His breast.

She faded from our vision,
　　Like a thing of love and light;
But we feel she lives for ever,
　　A spirit pure and bright.

REPORT

I heard, my young friend
　　You were seeking a wife,
A woman to make
　　Your companion for life.

Now, if you are seeking
　　A wife for your youth,
Let this be your aim, then—
　　Seek a woman of truth.

She may not have talents,
　　With greatness combined,
Her gifts may be humble,
　　Of person and mind:

But if she be constant,
　　And gentle, and true,
Believe me my friend,
　　She's the woman for you!

Oh! wed not for beauty,
　　Though fair is the prize;
It may pall when you grasp it,
　　And fade in your eyes.

Let gold not allure you,
  Let wealth not attract;
With a house full of treasure,
  A woman may lack.

Let her habits be frugal,
  Her hands not afraid
To work in her household
  Or follow her trade.

Let her language be modest,
  Her actions discreet;
Her manners refined,
  And free from deceit.

Now if such you should find,
  In your journey through life,
Just open your mind,
  And make her your wife.

ADVICE TO THE GIRLS

Nay, do not blush! I only heard
  You had a mind to marry;
I thought I'd speak a friendly word,
  So just one moment tarry.

Wed not a man whose merit lies
  In things of outward show,
In raven hair or flashing eyes,
  That please your fancy so.

But marry one who's good and kind,
  And free from all pretence;
Who, if without a gifted mind,
  At least has common sense.

SAVED BY FAITH

"She said, if I may but touch his clothes, I shall be whole."

Life to her no brightness brought,
    Pale and striken was her brow,
Till a bright and joyous thought
    Lit the darkness of her woe.

Long had sickness on her preyed,
    Strength from every nerve had gone;
Skill and art could give no aid:
    Thus her weary life passed on.

Like a sad and mournful dream,
    Daily felt she life depart,
Hourly knew the vital stream
    Left the fountain of her heart.

He who lull'd the storm to rest,
    Cleans'd the lepers, raised the dead,
Whilst a crowd around him press'd,
    Near that suffering one did tread.

Nerv'd by blended hope and fear,
    Reasoned thus her anxious heart;
"If to touch Him I draw near,
    All my suffering shall depart.

"While the crowd around him stand,
    I will touch," the sufferer said;
Forth she reached her timid hand—
    As she touched her sickness fled.

"Who hath touched me?" Jesus cried;
    "Virtue from my body gone."
From the crowd a voice replied,
    "Why inquire in such a throng?"

Faint with fear through every limb,
    Yet too grateful to deny,
Tremblingly she knelt to him,
    "Lord!" she answered, "it was I!"

Kindly, gently, Jesus said—
    Words like balm unto her soul—
"Peace upon thy life be shed!
    "Child! thy faith has made thee whole!"

DIED OF STARVATION

They forced him into prison,
    Because he begged for bread;
"My wife is starving—dying!"
    In vain the poor man plead.*

They forced him into prison,
    Strong bars enclosed the walls,
While the rich and proud were feasting
    Within their sumptuous halls.

He'd striven long with anguish,
    Had wrestled with despair;
But his weary heart was breaking
    'Neath its crushing load of care.

And he prayed them in that prison,
    "Oh, let me seek my wife!"
For he knew that want was feeding
    On the remnant of her life.

That night his wife lay moaning
    Upon her bed in pain;
Hunger gnawing at her vitals,
    Fever scorching through her brain.

* See this case, as touchingly related in *Oliver Twist*, by Dickens.

She wondered at his tarrying,
    He was not wont to stay;
'Mid hunger, pain and watching,
    The moments waned away.

Sadly crouching by the embers,
    Her famished children lay;
And she longed to gaze upon them,
    As her spirit passed away.

But the embers were too feeble,
    She could not see each face,
So she clasped her arms around them—
    'Twas their mother's last embrace.

They loosed him from his prison,
    As a felon from his chain;
Though his strength was hunger bitten,
    He sought his home again.

Just as her spirit linger'd
    On Time's receding shore,
She heard his welcome footstep
    On the threshold of the door.

He was faint and spirit-broken,
    But, rousing from despair,
He clasped her icy fingers,
    As she breathed her dying prayer.

With a gentle smile and blessing,
    Her spirit winged its flight,
As the morn, in all its glory,
    Bathed the world in dazzling light.

There was weeping, bitter weeping,
    In the chamber of the dead,
For well the stricken husband knew
    She had died for want of bread.

A MOTHER'S HEROISM

When the noble mother of Lovejoy heard of her son's death, she said, "It is well! I had rather he should die so than desert his principles."

The murmurs of a distant strife
  Fell on a mother's ear;
Her son had yielded up his life,
  Mid scenes of wrath and fear.

They told her how he'd spent his breath
  In pleading for the dumb,
And how the glorious martyr wreath
  Her child had nobly won.

They told her of his courage high,
  Mid brutal force and might;
How he had nerved himself to die
  In battling for the right.

It seemed as if a fearful storm
  Swept wildly round her soul;
A moment, and her fragile form
  Bent 'neath its fierce control.

From lip and brow the color fled—
  But light flashed to her eye:
" 'Tis well! 'tis well!" the mother said,
  "That thus my child should die.

" 'Tis well that, to his latest breath,
  He plead for liberty;
Truth nerved him for the hour of death,
  And taught him how to die.

"It taught him how to cast aside
  Earth's honors and renown;
To trample on her fame and pride,
  And win a martyr's crown."

THE FUGITIVE'S WIFE

It was my sad and weary lot
    To toil in slavery;
But one thing cheered my lowly cot—
    My husband was with me.

One evening, as our children played
    Around our cabin door,
I noticed on his brow a shade
    I'd never seen before;

And in his eyes a gloomy night
    Of anguish and despair;—
I gazed upon their troubled light,
    To read the meaning there.

He strained me to his heaving heart—
    My own beat wild with fear;
I knew not, but I sadly felt
    There might be evil near.

He vainly strove to cast aside
    The tears that fell like rain:—
Too frail, indeed, is manly pride,
    To strive with grief and pain.

Again he clasped me to his breast,
    And said that we must part:
I tried to speak—but, oh! it seemed
    An arrow reached my heart.

"Bear not," I cried, "unto your grave,
    The yoke you've borne from birth;
No longer live a helpless slave,
    The meanest thing on earth!"

THE CONTRAST

They scorned her for her sinning,
  Spoke harshly of her fall,
Nor let the hand of mercy
  To break her hated thrall.

The dews of meek repentance
  Stood in her downcast eye:
Would no one heed her anguish?
  All pass her coldly by?

From the cold, averted glances
  Of each reproachful eye,
She turned aside, heart-broken,
  And laid her down to die.

And where was he, who sullied
  Her once unspotted name;
Who lured her from life's brightness
  To agony and shame?

Who left her on life's billows,
  A wrecked and ruined thing;
Who brought the winter of despair
  Upon Hope's blooming spring?

Through the halls of wealth and fashion
  In gaiety and pride,
He was leading to the altar
  A fair and lovely bride!

None scorned him for his sinning,
  Few saw it through his gold;
His crimes were only foibles,
  And these were gently told.

Before him rose a vision,
    A maid of beauty rare;
Then a pale, heart-broken woman,
    The image of despair.

Next came a sad procession,
    With many a sob and tear;
A widow'd, childless mother
    Totter'd by an humble bier.

The vision quickly faded,
    The sad, unwelcome sight;
But his lip forgot its laughter,
    And his eye its careless light.

A moment, and the flood-gates
    Of memory opened wide;
And remorseful recollection
    Flowed like a lava tide.

That widow's wail of anguish
    Seemed strangely blending there,
And mid the soft lights floated
    That image of despair.

THE PRODIGAL'S RETURN

He came—a wanderer; years of sin
    Had blanched his blooming cheek,
Telling a tale of strife within,
    That words might vainly speak.

His feet were bare, his garments torn,
    His brow was deathly white;
His heart was bleeding, crushed and worn,
    His soul had felt a blight.

His father saw him; pity swept
    And yearn'd through every vein;
He ran and clasp'd his child, and wept,
    Murm'ring, "He lives again!"

"Father, I've come, but not to claim
    Aught from thy love or grace;
I come, a child of guilt and shame,
    To beg a servant's place."

"Enough! enough!" the father said,
    "Bring robes of princely cost!"—
The past with all its shadows fled,
    For now was found the lost.

"Put shoes upon my poor child's feet,
    With rings his hand adorn,
And bid my house his coming greet
    With music, dance and song."

Oh! Saviour, mid this world of strife,
    When wayward here we roam,
Conduct us to the paths of life,
    And guide us safely home.

Then in thy holy courts above,
    Thy praise our lips shall sound,
While angels join our song of love,
    That we, the lost are found!

EVA'S FAREWELL

Farewell, father! I am a dying,
    Going to the "glory land,"
Where the sun is ever shining,
    And the zephyr's ever bland.

Where the living fountains flowing,
　　Quench the pining spirit's thirst;
Where the tree of life is growing,
　　Where the crystal fountains burst.

Father! hear that music holy
　　Floating from the spirit land!
At the pearly gates of glory,
　　Radiant angels waiting stand.

Father! kiss your dearest Eva,
　　Press her cold and clammy hand,
Ere the glittering hosts receive her,
　　Welcome to their cherub band.

THE TENNESSEE HERO

"He had heard his comrades plotting to obtain their liberty,
and rather than betray them he received 750 lashes and died."

He stood before the savage throng,
　　The base and coward crew;
A tameless light flashed from his eye,
　　His heart beat firm and true.

He was the hero of his band,
　　The noblest of them all;
Though fetters galled his weary limbs,
　　His spirit spurned their thrall.

And towered, in its manly might,
　　Above the murderous crew.
Oh! liberty had nerved his heart,
　　And every pulse beat true.

"Now tell us," said the savage troop,
"And life thy gain shall be!
Who are the men that plotting, say—
'They must and will be free!' "

Oh, could you have seen the hero then,
As his lofty soul arose,
And his dauntless eyes defiance flashed
On his mean and craven foes!

"I know the men who would be free;
They are the heroes of your land;
But death and torture I defy,
Ere I betray that band.

"And what! oh, what is life to me,
Beneath your base control?
Nay! do your worst. Ye have no chains
To bind my free-born soul."

They brought the hateful lash and scourge,
With murder in each eye.
But a solemn vow was on his lips—
He had resolved to die.

Yes, rather than betray his trust,
He'd meet a death of pain;
'Twas sweeter far to meet it thus
Than wear a treason stain!

Like storms of wrath, of hate and pain,
The blows rained thick and fast;
But the monarch soul kept true
Till the gates of life were past.

And the martyr spirit fled
To the throne of God on high,
And showed his gaping wounds
Before the unslumbering eye.

FREE LABOR

I wear an easy garment,
    O'er it no toiling slave
Wept tears of hopeless anguish,
    In his passage to the grave.

And from its ample folds
    Shall rise no cry to God,
Upon its warp and woof shall be
    No stain of tears and blood.

Oh, lightly shall it press my form,
    Unladen with a sigh,
I shall not 'mid its rustling hear,
    Some sad despairing cry.

This fabric is too light to bear
    The weight of bondsmen's tears,
I shall not in its texture trace
    The agony of years.

Too light to bear a smother'd sigh,
    From some lorn woman's heart,
Whose only wreath of household love
    Is rudely torn apart.

Then lightly shall it press my form,
    Unburden'd by a sigh;
And from its seams and folds shall rise,
    No voice to pierce the sky,

And witness at the throne of God,
    In language deep and strong,
That I have nerv'd Oppression's hand,
    For deeds of guilt and wrong.

LINES

At the Portals of the Future
    Full of madness, guilt and gloom,
Stood the hateful form of Slavery,
    Crying, "Give, Oh! give me room—

"Room to smite the earth with cursing,
    Room to scatter, rend and slay,
From the trembling mother's bosom
    Room to tear her child away;

"Room to trample on the manhood
    Of the country far and wide;
Room to spread o'er every Eden
    Slavery's scorching lava-tide."

Pale and trembling stood the Future,
    Quailing 'neath his frown of hate,
As he grasped with bloody clutches
    The great keys of Doom and Fate.

In his hand he held a banner
    All festooned with blood and tears:
'Twas a fearful ensign, woven
    With the grief and wrong of years.

On his brow he wore a helmet
    Decked with strange and cruel art;
Every jewel was a life-drop
    Wrung from some poor broken heart.

Though her cheek was pale and anxious,
    Wet, with look and brow sublime,
By the pale and trembling Future
    Stood the Crisis of our time.

And from many a throbbing bosom
　　Came the words in fear and gloom,
"Tell us, oh! thou coming Crisis,
　　What shall be our country's doom?

"Shall the wings of dark destruction
　　Brood and hover o'er our land,
Till we trace the steps of ruin
　　By their blight, from strand to strand?"

With a look and voice prophetic
　　Spake the solemn Crisis then:
"I have only mapped the future
　　For the erring sons of men.

"If ye strive for Truth and Justice,
　　If ye battle for the Right,
Ye shall lay you. hands all strengthened
　　On God's robe of love and light;

"But if ye trample on His children,
　　To his ear will float each groan,
Jar the cords that bind them to Him,
　　And they'll vibrate at his ʰhrone.

"And the land that forges fetᵤᵣrs,
　　Binds the weak and poor in chains,
Must in blood or tears of sorrow
　　Wash away her guilty stains."

THE DISMISSAL OF TYNG

"We have but three words to say, 'served him right.' "
　　　　　　　　　　　Church Journal (Episcopal)

Served him right! How could he dare
　　To touch the idol of our day?

What if its shrine be red with blood?
    Why, let him turn his eyes away.

Who dares dispute our right to bind
    With galling chains the weak and poor?
To starve and crush the deathless mind,
    Or hunt the slave from door to door?

Who dares dispute our right to sell
    The mother from her weeping child?
To hush with ruthless stripes and blows
    Her shrieks and sobs of anguish wild?

'Tis right to plead for heathen lands,
    To send the Bible to their shores,
And then to make, for power and pelf,
    A race of heathens at our door.

What holy horror filled our hearts—
    It shook our church from dome to nave—
Our cheeks grew pale with pious dread,
    To hear him breathe the name of slave.

Upon our Zion, fair and strong,
    His words fell like a fearful blight;
We turned him from our silent fold;
    And this we did to "serve him right."

THE SLAVE MOTHER,
a Tale of the Ohio

I have but four, the treasures of my soul,
    They lay like doves around my heart;
I tremble lest some cruel hand
    Should tear my household wreaths apart.

My baby girl, with childish glance,
  Looks curious in my anxious eye,
She little knows that for her sake
  Deep shadows round my spirit lie.

My playful boys could I forget,
  My home might seem a joyous spot,
But with their sunshine mirth I blend
  The darkness of their future lot.

And thou my babe, my darling one,
  My last, my loved, my precious child,
Oh! when I think upon thy doom
  My heart grows faint and then throbs wild.

The Ohio's bridged and spanned with ice,
  The northern star is shining bright,
I'll take the nestlings of my heart
  And search for freedom by its light.

Winter and night were on the earth,
  And feebly moaned the shivering trees,
A sigh of winter seemed to run
  Through every murmur of the breeze.

She fled, and with her children all,
  She reached the stream and crossed it o'er,
Bright visions of deliverance came
  Like dreams of plenty to the poor.

Dreams! vain dreams, heroic mother,
  Give all thy hopes and struggles o'er,
The pursuer is on thy track,
  And the hunter at thy door.

Judea's refuge cities had power
  To shelter, shield and save,

E'en Rome had altars, 'neath whose shade
    Might crouch the wan and weary slave.

But Ohio had no sacred fane,
    To human rights so consecrated,
Where thou may'st shield thy hapless ones
    From their darkly gathering fate.

Then, said the mournful mother,
    If Ohio cannot save,
I will do a deed for freedom,
    Shalt find each child a grave.

I will save my precious children
    From their darkly threatened doom,
I will hew their path to freedom
    Through the portals of the tomb.

A moment in the sunlight,
    She held a glimmering knife,
The next moment she had bathed it
    In the crimson fount of life.

They snatched away the fatal knife,
    Her boys shrieked wild with dread;
The baby girl was pale and cold,
    They raised it up, the child was dead.

Sends this deed of fearful daring
    Through my country's heart no thrill,
Do the icy hands of slavery
    Every pure emotion chill?

Oh! if there is any honor,
    Truth or justice in the land,
Will ye not, us men and Christians,
    On the side of freedom stand?

RIZPAH, THE DAUGHTER OF AI

Tidings! sad tidings for the daughter of Ai,
They are bearing her prince and loved away,
Destruction falls like a mournful pall
On the fallen house of ill-fated Saul.

And Rizpah hears that her loved must die,
But she hears it all with a tearless eye;
And clasping her hand with grief and dread
She meekly bows her queenly head.

The blood has left her blanching cheek,
Her quivering lips refuse to speak,
Oh! grief like hers has learned no tone—
A world of grief is all its own.

But the deed is done, and the hand is stay'd
That havoc among the brethren made,
And Rizpah takes her lowly seat
To watch the princely dead at her feet.

The jackall crept out with a stealthy tread,
To batten and feast on the noble dead;
The vulture bore down with a heavy wing
To dip his beak in life's stagnant spring.

The hyena heard the jackall's howl,
And he bounded forth with a sullen growl,
When Rizpah's shriek rose on the air
Like a tone from the caverns of despair.

She sprang from her sad and lowly seat,
For a moment her heart forgot to beat,
And the blood rushes up to her marble cheek
And a flash to her eye so sad and meek.

The vulture paused in his downward flight,
As she raised her form to its queenly height,

The hyena's eye had a horrid glare
As he turned again to his desert lair.

The jackall slunk back with a quickened tread,
From his cowardly search of Rizpah's dead;
Unsated he turned from the noble prey,
Subdued by the glance of the daughter of Ai.

Of grief! that a mother's heart should know,
Such a weary weight of consuming wo,
For seldom if ever earth has known
Such love as the daughter of Ai hath known.

RUTH AND NAOMI

"Turn my daughters, full of wo,
   Is my heart so sad and lone?
Leave me children—I would go
   To my loved and distant home.

"From my bosom death has torn
   Husband, children, all my stay,
Left me not a single one,
   For my life's declining day.

"Want and wo surround my way,
   Grief and famine where I tread;
In my native land they say
   God is giving Jacob bread."

Naomi ceased, her daughters wept,
   Their yearning hearts were filled;
Falling upon her withered neck,
   Their grief in tears distill'd.

Like rain upon a blighted tree,
   The tears of Orpah fell
Kissing the pale and quivering lip,
   She breathed her sad farewell.

But Ruth stood up, on her brow
    There lay a heavenly calm;
And from her lips came, soft and low
    Words like a holy charm.

"I will not leave thee, on thy brow
    Are lines of sorrow, age and care;
They form is bent, thy step is slow,
    They bosom stricken, lone and sear.

"Oh! when thy heart and home were glad,
    I freely shared thy joyous lot;
And now that heart is lone and sad,
    Cease to entreat—I'll leave thee not.

"Oh! if a lofty palace proud
    Thy future home shall be;
Where sycophants around thee crowd,
    I'll share that home with thee.

"And if on earth the humblest spot,
    Thy future home shall prove;
I'll bring into thy lonely lot
    The wealth of woman's love.

"Go where thou wilt, my steps are there,
    Our path in life is one;
Thou hast no lot I will not share,
    'Till life itself be done.

"My country and my home for thee,
    I freely, willingly resign,
Thy people shall my people be,
    Thy God he shall be mine.

"Then, mother dear, entreat me not
    To turn from following thee;
My heart is nerved to share thy lot,
    Whatever that may be."

MOSES
A STORY OF THE NILE

THE PARTING
Chapter I

Moses

Kind and gracious princess, more than friend,
I've come to thank thee for thy goodness,
And to breathe into thy generous ears
My last and sad farewell. I go to join
The fortunes of my race, and to put aside
All other bright advantages, save
The approval of my conscience and the meed
Of rightly doing.

Princess

What means, my son, this strange election?
What wild chimera floats across thy mind?
What sudden impulse moves thy soul? Thou who
Hast only trod the court of kings, why seek
Instead the paths of labor? Thou, whose limbs
Have known no other grab than that which well
Befits our kingly state, why rather choose
The badge of servitude and toil?

Moses

Let me tell thee, gracious princess; 'tis no
Sudden freak nor impulse wild that moves my mind.
I feel an earnest purpose binding all
My soul until a strong resolve, which bids

34

Me put aside all other ends and aims,
Until the hour shall come when God—the God
Our fathers loved and worshipped—shall break our chains,
And lead our willing feet to freedom.

Princess

Listen to me, Moses: thou art young,
And the warm blood of youth flushes thy veins
Like generous wine; thou wearest thy manhood
Like a crown; but what king e'er cast
His diadem in the dust, to be trampled
Down by every careless foot? Thou hast
Bright dreams and glowing hopes; could'st thou not live
Them out as well beneath the radiance
Of our throne as in the shadow of those
Bondage-darkened huts?

Moses

Within those darkened huts my mother plies her tasks,
My father bends to unrequited toil;
And bitter tears moisten the bread my brethren eat.
And when I gaze upon their cruel wrongs
The very purple on my limbs seems drenched
With blood, the warm blood of my own kindred race;
And then thy richest viands pall upon my taste,
And discord jars in every tone of song.
I cannot live in pleasure while they faint
In pain.

Princess

How like a dream the past floats back: it seems
But yesterday when I lay tossing upon

My couch of pain, a torpor creeping through
Each nerve, a fever coursing through my veins.
And there I lay, dreaming of lilies fair,
Of lotus flowers and past delights, and all
The bright, glad hopes, that give to early life
Its glow and flush; and thus day after day
Dragged its slow length along, until, one morn,
The breath of lilies, fainting on the air,
Floated into my room, and then I longed once more
To gaze upon the Nile, as on the face
Of a familiar friend, whose absence long
Had made a mournful void within the heart.
I summoned to my side my maids, and bade
Them place my sandals on my feet, and lead
Me to the Nile, where I might bathe my weary
Limbs within the cooling flood, and gather
Healing from the sacred stream.
I sought my favorite haunt, and, bathing, found
New tides of vigor coursing through my veins.
Refreshed, I sat me down to weave a crown of lotus leaves
And lilies fair, and while I sat in a sweet
Revery, dreaming of life and hope, I saw
A little wicker-basket hidden among
The flags and lilies of the Nile, and I called
My maidens and said, "Nillias and Osiris,
Bring me that little ark which floats beside
The stream." They ran and brought me a precious burden.
'Twas an ark woven with rushes and daubed
With slime, and in it lay a sleeping child;
His little hand amid his clustering curls,
And a bright flush upon his glowing cheek.
He wakened with a smile, and reached out his hand
To meet the welcome of the mother's kiss,
When strange faces met his gaze, and he drew back
With a grieved, wondering look, while disappointment

Shook the quivering lip that missed the mother's
Wonted kiss, and the babe lifted his voice and wept.
Then my heart yearned towards him, and I resolved
That I would brave my father's wrath and save
The child; but while I stood gazing upon
His wondrous beauty, I saw beside me
A Hebrew girl, her eyes bent on me
With an eager, questioning look, and drawing
Near, she timidly said, "Shall I call a nurse?"
I bade her go; she soon returned, and with her
Came a woman of the Hebrew race, whose
Sad, sweet, serious eyes seemed overflowing
With a strange and sudden joy. I placed the babe
Within her arms and said, "Nurse this child for me;"
And the babe nestled there like one at home,
While o'er the dimples of his face rippled
The brightest, sweetest smiles, and I was well
Content to leave him in her care; and well
Did she perform her part. When many days had
Passed she brought the child unto the palace;
And one morning, while I sat toying with
His curls and listening to the prattle of his
Untrained lips, my father, proud and stately,
Saw me bending o'er the child and said,
"Charmian, whose child is this? who of my lords
Calls himself father to this goodly child?
He surely must be a happy man."
        Then I said, "Father, he is mine. He is a
Hebrew child that I have saved from death." He
Suddenly recoiled, as if an adder
Had stung him, and said, "Charmian, take that
Child hence. How darest thou bring a member
Of that mean and servile race within my doors?
Nay, rather let me send for Nechos, whose
Ready sword shall rid me of his hateful presence."

Then kneeling at his feet, and catching
Hold of his royal robes, I said, "Not so,
Oh! honored father, he is mine; I snatched
Him from the hungry jaws of death, and foiled
The greedy crocodile of his prey; he has
Eaten bread within thy palace walls, and thy
Salt lies upon his fresh young lips; he has
A claim upon thy mercy."

       "Charmian," he said
"I have decreed that every man child of that
Hated race shall die. The oracles have said
The pyramids shall wane before their shadow.
And from them a star shall rise whose light shall
Spread over earth a baleful glow; and this is why
I root them from the land; their strength is weakness
To my throne. I shut them from the light lest they
Bring darkness to my kingdom. Now, Charmian,
Give me up the child, and let him die."
Then clasping the child closer to my heart,
I said, "The pathway to his life is through my own;
Around that life I throw my heart, a wall
Of living, loving clay." Dark as the thunder
Clouds of distant lands became my father's brow,
And his eyes flashed with the fierce lightnings
Of his wrath; but while I plead, with eager
Eyes upturned, I saw a sudden change come
Over him; his eyes beamed with unwonted
Tenderness, and he said, "Charmian, arise,
Thy prayer is granted; just then thy dead mother
Came to thine eyes, and the light of Asenath
Broke over thy face. Asenath was the light
Of my home; the star that faded out too
Suddenly from my dwelling, and left my life
To darkness, grief and pain, and for her sake,
Not thine, I'll spare the child." And thus I saved

Thee twice—once from the angry sword and once
From the devouring flood. Moses, thou art
Doubly mine; as such I claimed thee then, as such
I claim thee now. I've nursed no other child
Upon my knee, and pressed upon no other
Lips the sweetest kisses of my love, and now,
With rash and careless hand, thou dost thrust aside that love.
There was a painful silence, a silence
So hushed and still that you might have almost
Heard the hurried breathing of one and the quick
Throbbing of the other's heart: for Moses,
He was slow of speech, but she was eloquent
With words of tenderness and love, and had breathed
Her full heart into her lips; but there was
Firmness in the young man's choice, and he beat back
The opposition of her lips with the calm
Grandeur of his will, and again he essayed to speak.

Moses

Gracious lady, thou remembrest well
The Hebrew nurse to whom thou gavest thy foundling.
That woman was my mother; from her lips I
Learned the grand traditions of our race that float
With all their weird and solemn beauty, around
Our wrecked and blighted fortunes. How oft!
With kindling eye and glowing cheek, forgetful
Of the present pain, she would lead us through
The distant past: the past, hallowed by deeds
Of holy faith and lofty sacrifice.
How she would tell us of Abraham,
The father of our race, that he dwelt in Ur;
Of the Chaldees, and when the Chaldean king
Had called him to his sacrifice, that he
Had turned from his dumb idols to the living

God, and wandered out from kindred, home and race,
Led by his faith in God alone; and she would
Tell us,—(we were three,) my brother Aaron,
The Hebrew girl thou sentest to call a nurse,
And I, her last, her loved and precious child;
She would tell us that one day our father
Abraham heard a voice, bidding him offer
Up in sacrifice the only son of his
Beautiful and beloved Sarah; that the father's
Heart shrank not before the bitter test of faith,
But he resolved to give his son to God
As a burnt offering upon Moriah's mount;
That the uplifted knife glittered in the morning
Sun, when, sweeter than the music of a thousand
Harps, he heard a voice bidding him to stay his hand,
And spare the child; and how his faith, like gold
Tried in the fiercest fire, shone brighter through
Its fearful test. And then she would tell us
Of a promise, handed down from sire to son,
That God, the God our fathers loved and worshiped,
Would break our chains, and bring to us a great
Deliverance; that we should dwell in peace
Beneath our vines and palms, our flocks and herds
Increase, and joyful children crowd our streets;
And then she would lift her eyes unto the far
Off hills and tell us of the patriarchs
Of our line, who sleep in distant graves within
That promised land; and now I feel the hour
Draws near which brings deliverance to our race.

Princess

These are but the dreams of thy young fancy;
I cannot comprehend thy choice. I have heard
Of men who have waded through slaughter

To a throne; of proud ambitions, struggles
Fierce and wild for some imagined good; of men
Who have even cut in twain the crimson threads
That lay between them and a throne; but I
Never heard of men resigning ease for toil,
The splendor of a palace for the squalor
Of a hut, and casting down a diadem
To wear a servile badge.

                Sadly she gazed
Upon the fair young face lit with its lofty
Faith and high resolves—the dark prophetic eyes
Which seemed to look beyond the present pain
Unto the future greatness of his race.
As she stood before him in the warm
Loveliness of her ripened womanhood,
Her languid eyes glowed with unwonted fire,
And the bright tropical blood sent its quick
Flushes o'er the olive of her cheek, on which
Still lay the lingering roses of her girlhood.
Grief, wonder, and surprise flickered like shadows
O'er her face as she stood slowly crushing
With unconscious hand the golden tassels
Of her crimson robe. She had known life only
By its brightness, and could not comprehend
The grandeur of the young man's choice; but she
Felt her admiration glow before the earnest
Faith that tore their lives apart and led him
To another destiny. She had hoped to see
The crown of Egypt on his brow, the sacred
Leopard skin adorn his shoulders, and his seat
The throne of the proud Pharaoh's; but now her
Dream had faded out and left a bitter pang
Of anguish in its stead. And thus they parted,
She to brood in silence o'er her pain, and he
To take his mission from the hands of God

And lead his captive race to freedom.
With silent lips but aching heart she bowed
Her queenly head and let him pass, and he
Went forth to share the fortune of his race,
Esteeming that as better far than pleasures
Bought by sin and gilded o'er with vice.
And he had chosen well, for on his brow
God poured the chrism of a holy work.
And thus anointed he has stood a bright
Ensample through the changing centuries of time.

Chapter II

It was a great change from the splendor, light
And pleasure of a palace to the lowly huts
Of those who sighed because of cruel bondage.
                              As he passed
Into the outer courts of that proud palace,
He paused a moment just to gaze upon
The scenes 'mid which his early life had passed—
The pleasant haunts amid the fairest flowers,—
The fountains tossing on the air their silver spray—
The statues breathing music soft and low
To greet the first faint flushes of the morn,—
The obelisks that rose in lofty grandeur
From their stony beds—the sphynxes gaunt and grim,
With unsolved riddles on their lips—and all
The bright creation's painters art and sculptors
Skill had gathered in those regal halls, where mirth
And dance, and revelry, and song had chased
With careless feet the bright and fleeting hours.
He was leaving all; but no regrets came
Like a shadow o'er his mind, for he had felt
The quickening of a higher life, as if his
Soul had wings and he were conscious of their growth;

And yet there was a tender light in those
Dark eyes which looked their parting on the scenes
Of beauty, where his life had been a joyous
Dream enchanted with delight; but he trampled
On each vain regret as on a vanquished foe,
And went forth a strong man, girded with lofty
Purposes and earnest faith. He journeyed on
Till palaces and domes and lofty fanes,
And gorgeous temples faded from his sight,
And the lowly homes of Goshen came in view.
There he saw the women of his race kneading
Their tale of bricks; the sons of Abraham
Crouching beneath their heavy burdens. He saw
The increasing pallor on his sister's cheek,
The deepening shadows on his mother's brow,
The restless light that glowed in Aaron's eye,
As if a hidden fire were smouldering
In his brain; and bending o'er his mother
In a tender, loving way, he said, "Mother,
I've come to share the fortunes of my race,—
To dwell within these lowly huts,—to wear
The badge of servitude and toil, and eat
The bitter bread of penury and pain."
A sudden light beamed from his mother's eye,
And she said, "How's this, my son? but yesterday
Two Hebrews, journeying from On to Goshen,
Told us they had passed the temple of the Sun
But dared not enter, only they had heard
That it was a great day in On; that thou hadst
Forsworn thy kindred, tribe and race; hadst bowed
Thy knee to Egypt's vain and heathen worship:
Hadst denied the God of Abraham, of Isaac,
And of Jacob, and from henceforth wouldst
Be engrafted in Pharaoh's regal line,
And be called the son of Pharaoh's daughter.

When thy father Amram heard the cruel news
He bowed his head upon his staff and wept.
But I had stronger faith than that. By faith
I hid thee when the bloody hands of Pharaoh
Were searching 'mid our quivering heart strings,
Dooming our sons to death; by faith I wove
The rushes of thine ark and laid thee 'mid
The flags and lilies of the Nile, and saw
The answer to that faith when Pharaoh's daughter
Placed thee in my arms, and bade me nurse the child
For her: and by that faith sustained, I heard
As idle words the cruel news that stabbed
Thy father like a sword."

"The Hebrews did not hear aright; last week
There was a great day in On, from Esoan's gate
Unto the mighty sea; the princes, lords
And chamberlains of Egypt were assembled;
The temple of the sun was opened. Isis
And Osiris were unveiled before the people.
Apis and Orus were crowned with flowers;
Golden censers breathed their fragrance on the air;
The sacrifice was smoking on the altar;
The first fruits of the Nile lay on the tables
Of the sun; the music rose in lofty swells,
Then sank in cadences so soft and low
Till all the air grew tremulous with rapture.
The priests of On were there, with sacred palms
Within their hands and lotus leaves upon their
Brows; Pharaoh and his daughter sat waiting
In their regal chairs; all were ready to hear
Me bind my soul to Egypt, and to swear
Allegiance to her gods. The priests of On
Drew near to lay their hands upon my head
And bid me swear, "Now, by Osiris, judge
Of all the dead, and Isis, mother of us

All," that henceforth I'd forswear my kindred,
Tribe and race; would have no other gods
Than those of Egypt; would be engrafted
Into Pharaoh's royal line, and be called
The son of Pharaoh's daughter. Then, mother
Dear, I lived the past again. Again I sat
Beside thee, my lips apart with childish
Wonder, my eyes uplifted to thy
Glowing face, and my young soul gathering
Inspiration from thy words. Again I heard
Thee tell the grand traditions of our race,
The blessed hopes and glorious promises
That weave their golden threads among the sombre
Tissues of our lives, and shimmer still amid
The gloom and shadows of our lot. Again
I heard thee tell of Abraham, with his constant
Faith and earnest trust in God, unto whom
The promise came that in his seed should all
The nations of the earth be blessed. Of Isaac
Blessing with disappointed lips his first born son,
From whom the birthright had departed. Of Jacob,
With his warm affections and his devious ways,
Flying before the wrath of Esau; how he
Slumbered in the wild, and saw amid his dreams
A ladder reaching to the sky, on which God's
Angels did descend, and waking with a solemn
Awe o'ershadowing all, his soul exclaimed, "How
Dreadful is this place. Lo! God is here, and I
Knew it not." Of Joseph, once a mighty prince
Within this land, who shrank in holy horror
From the soft white hand that beckoned him to sin;
Whose heart, amid the pleasures, pomp and pride
Of Egypt, was ever faithful to his race,
And when his life was trembling on its frailest chord
He turned his dying eyes to Canaan, and made

His brethren swear that they would make his grave
Among the patriarchs of his line, because
Machpelah's cave, where Abraham bowed before
The sons of Heth, and bought a place to lay
His loved and cherished dead, was dearer to his
Dying heart than the proudest tomb amid
The princely dead of Egypt.
     Then, like the angels, mother dear, who met
Our father Jacob on his way, thy words
Came back as messengers of light to guide
My steps, and I refused to be called the son
Of Pharaoh's daughter. I saw the priests of On
Grow pale with fear, an ashen terror creeping
O'er the Princess' face, while Pharaoh's brow grew
Darker than the purple of his cloak. But I
Endured, as seeing him who hides his face
Behind the brightness of his glory.
And thus I left the pomp and pride of Egypt
To cast my lot upon the people of my race."

FLIGHT INTO MIDIAN
Chapter III

The love of Moses for his race soon found
A stern expression. Pharaoh was building
A pyramid; ambitious, cold and proud,
He scrupled not at means to gain his ends.
When he feared the growing power of Israel
He stained his hands in children's blood, and held
A carnival of death in Goshen; but now
He wished to hand his name and memory
Down unto the distant ages, and instead
Of lading that memory with the precious
Fragrance of the kindest deeds and words, he

Essayed to write it out in stone, as cold
And hard, and heartless as himself.
                              And Israel was
The fated race to whom the cruel tasks
Were given. Day after day a cry of wrong
And anguish, some dark deed of woe and crime,
Came to the ear of Moses, and he said,
"These reports are ever harrowing my soul;
I will go unto the fields where Pharaoh's
Officers exact their labors, and see
If these things be so—if they smite the feeble
At their tasks, and goad the aged on to toils
Beyond their strength—if neither age nor sex
Is spared the cruel smiting of their rods."
And Moses went to see his brethren.
                              'Twas eventide,
And the laborers were wending their way
Unto their lowly huts. 'Twas a sad sight,—
The young girls walked without the bounding steps
Of youth, with faces prematurely old,
As if the rosy hopes and sunny promises
Of life had never flushed their cheeks with girlish
Joy; and there were men whose faces seemed to say
We bear our lot in hopeless pain, we've bent unto
Our burdens until our shoulders fit them,
And as slaves we crouch beneath our servitude
And toil. But there were men whose souls were cast
In firmer moulds, men with dark secretive eyes,
Which seemed to say, to-day we bide our time,
And hide our wrath in every nerve, and only
Wait a fitting hour to strike the hands that press
Us down. Then came the officers of Pharaoh;
They trod as lords, their faces flushed with pride
And insolence, watching the laborers

Sadly wending their way from toil to rest.
And Moses' heart swelled with a mighty pain; sadly
Musing, he sought a path that led him
From the busy haunts of men. But even there
The cruel wrong trod in his footsteps; he heard
A heavy groan, then harsh and bitter words,
And, looking back, he saw an officer
Of Pharaoh smiting with rough and cruel hand
An aged man. Then Moses' wrath o'erflowed
His lips, and every nerve did tremble
With a sense of wrong, and bounding forth he
Cried unto the smiter, "Stay thy hand; seest thou
That aged man? His head is whiter than our
Desert sands; his limbs refuse to do thy
Bidding because the cruel tasks have drained
Away their strength." The Egyptian raised his eyes
With sudden wonder; who was this that dared dispute
His power? Only a Hebrew youth. His
Proud lip curved in scornful anger, and he
Waved a menace with his hand, saying, "Back
To the task base slave, nor dare resist the will
Of Pharaoh." Then Moses' wrath o'erleaped the bounds
Of prudence, and with a heavy blow he felled
The smiter to the earth, and Israel had
One tyrant less. Moses saw the mortal paleness
Chase the flushes from the Egyptian's face,
The whitening lips that breathed no more defiance
And the relaxing tension of the well knit limbs.
And when he knew that he was dead, he hid
Him in the sand and left him to his rest.
                              Another day Moses walked
Abroad, and saw two brethren striving
For mastery; and then his heart grew full
Of tender pity. They were brethren, sharers
Of a common wrong; should not their wrongs more

Closely bind their hearts, and union, not division,
Be their strength? And feeling thus, he said, "Ye
Are brethren, wherefore do ye strive together?"
But they threw back his words in angry tones
And asked if he had come to judge them, and would
Mete to them the fate of the Egyptians?
Then Moses knew the sand had failed to keep
His secret, that his life no more was safe
In Goshen, and he fled unto the deserts
Of Arabia and became a shepherd
For the priest of Midian.

Chapter IV

Men grow strong in action, but in solitude
Their thoughts are ripened. Like one who cuts away
The bridge on which he has walked in safety
To the other side, so Moses cut off all retreat
To Pharaoh's throne, and did choose the calling
Most hateful to an Egyptian; he became
A shepherd, and led his flocks and herds amid
The solitude and wilds of Midian, where he
Nursed in silent loneliness his earnest faith
In God and a constant love for kindred, tribe
And race. Years stole o'er him, but they took
No atom from his strength, nor laid one heavy weight
Upon his shoulders. The down upon his face
Had ripened to a heavy beard; the fire
That glowed within his youthful eye had deepened
To a calm and steady light, and yet his heart
Was just as faithful to his race as when he had
Stood in Pharaoh's courts and bade farewell
Unto his daughter.
There was a look of patient waiting on his face,
A calm, grand patience, like one who had lifted

Up his eyes to God and seen, with meekened face,
The wings of some great destiny o'ershadowing
All his life with strange and solemn glory.
But the hour came when he must pass from thought
To action.—when the hope of many years
Must reach its grand fruition, and Israel's
Great deliverance dawn. It happened thus:
One day, as Moses led his flocks, he saw
A fertile spot skirted by desert sands,—
A pleasant place for flocks and herds to nip
The tender grass and rest within its shady nooks;
And as he paused and turned, he saw a bush with fire
Aglow; from root to stem a lambent flame
Sent up its jest and sprays of purest light,
And yet the bush, with leaves uncrisped, uncurled,
Was just as green and fresh as if the breath
Of early spring were kissing every leaf.
Then Moses said, "I'll turn aside to see
This sight," and as he turned he heard a voice
Bidding him lay his sandals by, for Lo! he
Stood on holy ground. Then Moses bowed his head
Upon his staff and spread his mantle o'er
His face, lest he should see the dreadful majesty
Of God; and there, upon that lonely spot,
By Horeb's mount, his shrinking hands received
The burden of his God, which bade him go
To Egypt's guilty king, and bid him let
The oppressed go free.
                                    Commissioned thus
He gathered up his flocks and herds and sought
The tents of Jethro, and said "I pray thee
Let me go and see if yet my kindred live;"
And Jethro bade him go in peace, nor sought
To throw himself across the purpose of his soul.
Yet there was tender parting in that home;

There were moistened eyes, and quivering lips,
And lingering claspings of the parting hand, as Jethro
And his daughters stood within the light of that
Clear morn, and gave to Moses and his wife
And sons their holy wishes and their sad farewells.
For he had been a son and brother in that home
Since first with manly courtesy he had filled
The empty pails of Reuel's daughters, and found
A shelter 'neath his tent when flying from
The wrath of Pharaoh.

                They journeyed on,
Moses, Zipporah and sons, she looking back
With tender love upon the home she had left,
With all its precious memories crowding round
Her heart, and he with eager eyes tracking
His path across the desert, longing once more
To see the long-lost faces of his distant home,
The loving eyes so wont to sun him with their
Welcome, and the aged hands that laid upon
His youthful head their parting blessing. They
Journeyed on till morning's flush and noonday
Splendor gilded into the softened, mellowed
Light of eve, and the purple mists were deep'ning
On the cliffs and hills, when Horeb, dual
Crowned, arose before him; and there he met
His brother Aaron, sent by God to be
His spokesman and to bear him company
To Pharaoh. Tender and joyous was their greeting.
They talked of home and friends until the lighter
Rapple of their thoughts in deeper channels flowed;
And then they talked of Israel's bondage,
And the great deliverance about to dawn
Upon the fortunes of their race; and Moses
Told him of the burning bush, and how the message
Of his God was trembling on his lips. And thus

They talked until the risen moon had veiled
The mount in soft and silvery light; and then
They rested until morn, and rising up, refreshed
From sleep, pursued their way until they reached
The land of Goshen, and gathered up the elders
Of their race, and told them of the message
Of their Father's God. Then eager lips caught up
The words of hope and passed the joyful news
Around, and all the people bowed their heads
And lifted up their hearts in thankfulness
To God.
                            That same day
Moses sought an audience with the king. He found
Him on his throne surrounded by the princes
Of his court, who bowed in lowly homage
At his feet. And Pharaoh heard with curving lip
And flushing cheek the message of the Hebrew's God
Then asked in cold and scornful tones, "Has
Israel a God, and if so where has he dwelt
For ages? As the highest priest of Egypt
I have prayed to Isis, and the Nile has
Overflowed her banks and filled the land
With plenty, but these poor slaves have cried unto
Their God, they crept in want and sorrow
To their graves. Surely, Mizraim's God is strong
And Israel's is weak; then wherefore should
I heed his voice, or at this bidding break
A single yoke?" Thus reasoned that proud king,
And turned a deafened ear unto the words
Of Moses and his brother, and yet he felt
Strangely awed before their presence, because
They stood as men who felt the grandeur
Of their mission, and thought not of themselves
But of their message.

Chapter V

On the next day Pharaoh called a council
Of his mighty men, and before them laid
The message of the brethren: then Amorphel,
Keeper of the palace and nearest lord
Unto the king, arose, and bending low
Before the throne, prayed leave to speak a word.
Amorphel was a crafty, treacherous man,
With oily lips well versed in flattery
And curtly speech, a supple reed ready
To bend before his royal master's lightest
Breath—Pharaoh's willing tool. He said
"Gracious king, thou hast been too lenient
With these slaves; light as their burdens are, they
Fret and chafe beneath them. They are idle
And the blood runs riot in their veins. Now
If thou would'st have those people dwell in peace,
Increase, I pray thee, their tasks and add unto
Their burdens; if they faint beneath their added
Tasks, they will have less time to plot sedition
And revolt."

Then Rhadma, oldest lord in Pharaoh's court,
Arose. He was an aged man, whose white
And heavy beard hung low upon his breast,
Yet there was a hard cold glitter in his eye,
And on his face a proud and evil look.
He had been a servant to the former king,
And wore his signet ring upon his hand.
He said, "I know this Moses well. Fourscore
Years ago Princess Charmian found him
By the Nile and rescued him from death, and did
Choose him as her son, and had him versed in all

The mysteries and lore of Egypt. But blood
Will tell, and this base slave, with servile blood
Within his veins, would rather be a servant
Than a prince, and so, with rude and reckless hand,
He thrust aside the honors of our dear
Departed king. Pharaoh was justly wroth,
But for his daughter's sake he let the trespass
Pass. But one day this Moses slew an Egyptian
In his wrath, and then the king did seek his life;
But he fled, it is said, unto the deserts
Of Arabia, and became a shepherd for the priest
Of Midian. But now, instead of leading flocks
And herds, he aspires to lead his captive race
To freedom. These men mean mischief; sedition
And revolt are in their plans. Decree, I pray thee,
That these men shall gather their own straw
And yet their tale of bricks shall be the same."
And these words pleased Pharaoh well, and all his
Lords chimed in with one accord. And Pharaoh
Wrote the stern decree and sent it unto Goshen—
That the laborers should gather their own straw,
And yet they should not 'minish of their tale of bricks.
                        'Twas a sad day in Goshen;
The king's decree hung like a gloomy pall
Around their homes. The people fainted 'neath
Their added tasks, then cried unto the king,
That he would ease their burdens; but he hissed
A taunt into their ears and said, "Ye are
Idle, and your minds are filled with vain
And foolish thoughts; get you unto your tasks,
And ye shall not 'minish of your tale of bricks."
                        And they turned their eyes
Reproachfully to Moses and his brother,
And laid the cruel blame upon their shoulders.

'Tis an old story now, but then 'twas new
Unto the brethren,—how God's anointed ones
Must walk with bleeding feet the paths that turn
To lines of living light; how hands that bring
Salvation in their palms are pierced with cruel
Nails, and lips that quiver first with some great truth
Are steeped in bitterness and tears, and brows
Now bright beneath the aureola of God,
Have bent beneath the thorny crowns of earth.
                              There was no hope for Israel,
But they did not see the golden fringes
Of their coming morn; they only saw the cold,
Grey sky, and fainted 'neath the cheerless gloom.

Moses sought again the presence of the king:
And Pharaoh's brow grew dark with wrath,
And rising up in angry haste, he said
Defiantly, "If thy God be great, show
Us some sign or token of his power."
Then Moses threw his rod upon the floor,
And it trembled with a sign of life;
The dark wood glowed, then changed into a thing
Of glistening scales and golden rings, and green
And brown and purple stripes; a hissing, hateful
Thing, that glared its fiery eye, and darting forth
From Moses' side, lay coiled and panting
At the monarch's feet. With wonder open-eyed
The king gazed on the changed rod, then called
For his magicians—wily men, well versed
In sinful lore—and bade them do the same.
And they, leagued with the powers of night, did
Also change their rods to serpents; then Moses'
Serpent darted forth, and with a startling hiss
And angry gulp, he swallowed the living things

That coiled along his path. And thus did Moses
Show that Israel's God had greater power
Than those dark sons of night.
                        But not by this alone
Did God his mighty power reveal: He changed
Their waters; every fountain, well and pool
Was red with blood, and lips, all parched with thirst,
Shrank back in horror from the crimson draughts.
And then the worshiped Nile grew full of life:
Millions of frogs swarmed from the stream—they clogged
The pathway of the priests and filled the sacred
Fanes, and crowded into Pharaoh's bed, and hopped
Into his trays of bread, and slumbered in his
Ovens and his pans.

There came another plague, of loathsome vermin;
They were gray and creeping things, that made
Their very clothes alive with dark and sombre
Spots—things of loathsome in the land, they did
Suspend the service of the temple; for no priest
Dared to lift his hand to any god with one
Of those upon him. And then the sky grew
Dark, as if a cloud were passing o'er its
Changeless blue; a buzzing sound broke o'er
The city, and the land was swarmed with flies.
The Murrain laid their cattle low; the hail
Cut off the first fruits of the Nile; the locusts
With their hungry jaws, destroyed the later crops,
And left the ground as brown and bare as if a fire
Had scorched it through.
                        Then angry blains
And fiery boils did blur the flesh of man
And beast; and then for three long days, nor saffron
Tint, nor crimson flush, nor soft and silvery light
Divided day from morn, nor told the passage

Of the hours; men rose not from their seats, but sat
In silent awe. That lengthened night lay like a burden
On the air,—a darkness one might almost gather
In his hand, it was so gross and thick. Then came
The last dread plague—the death of the first born
                     'Twas midnight,
And a startling shriek rose from each palace,
Home and hut of Egypt, save the blood-besprinkled homes
Of Goshen; the midnight seemed to shiver with a sense
Of dread, as if the mystic angel's wing
Had chilled the very air with horror.
Death! Death! was everywhere—in every home
A corpse—in every heart a bitter woe.
There were anxious fingerings for the pulse
That ne'er would throb again, and eager listenings
For some sound of life—a hurrying to and fro—
Then burning kisses on the cold lips
Of the dead, bitter partings, sad farewells,
And mournful sobs and piercing shrieks,
And deep and heavy groans throughout the length
And breadth of Egypt. 'Twas the last dread plague,
But it had snapped in twain the chains on which
The rust of ages lay, and Israel was freed;
Not only freed, but thrust in eager haste
From the land. Trembling men stood by, and longed
To see them gather up their flocks and herds,
And household goods, and leave the land; because they felt
That death stood at their doors as long as Israel
Lingered there; and they went forth in haste,
To tread the paths of freedom.

Chapter VI

But Pharaoh was strangely blind, and turning
From his first-born and his dead, with Egypt's wail

Scarce still upon his ear, he asked which way had
Israel gone? They told him that they journeyed
Towards the mighty sea, and were encamped
Near Baalzephen.
Then Pharaoh said, "the wilderness will hem them in,
The mighty sea will roll its barriers in front,
And with my chariots and my warlike men
I'll bring them back, or mete them out their graves."
                    Then Pharaoh's officers arose
And gathered up the armies of the king
And made his chariots ready for pursuit
With proud escutcheons blazoned to the sun,
In his chariot of ivory, pearl and gold,
Pharaoh rolled out of Egypt; and with him
Rode his mighty men, their banners floating
On the breeze, their spears and armor glittering
In the morning light; and Israel saw,
With fainting hearts, their old oppressors on their
Track: then women wept in hopeless terror;
Children hid their faces in their mothers' robes,
And strong men bowed their head in agony and dread;
And then a bitter, angry murmur rose,—
"Were there no graves in Egypt, that thou hast
Brought us here to die?"
Then Moses lifted up his face, aglow
With earnest faith in God, and bade their fainting hearts
Be strong and they should his salvation see.
"Stand still," said Moses to the fearful throng
Whose hearts were fainting in the wild, "Stand still."
Ah, that was Moses' word, but higher and greater
Came God's watchword for the hour, and not for that
Alone, but all the coming hours of time
"Speak ye unto the people and bid them
Forward go; stretch thy hand across the waters
And smite them with thy rod." And Moses smote

The restless sea; the waves stood up in heaps,
Then lay as calm and still as lips that
Had tasted death. The secret-loving sea
Laid bare her coral caves and iris-tinted
Floor; that wall of flood which lined the people's
Way was God's own wondrous masonry;
The signal pillar sent to guide them through the wild
Moved its dark shadow till it fronted Egypt's
Camp, but hung in fiery splendor, a light
To Israel's path. Madly rushed the hosts
Of Pharaoh upon the people's track, when
The solemn truth broke on them—that God
For Israel fought. With cheeks in terror
Blenching, and eyes astart with fear, "Let
Us flee," they cried, "from Israel, for their God
Doth fight against us; he is battling on their side."
They had trusted in their chariots, but now
That hope was vain; God had loosened every
Axle and unfastened every wheel, and each
Face did gather blackness and each heart stood still
With fear, as the livid lightnings glittered
And the thunder roared and muttered on the air,
And they saw the dreadful ruin that shuddered
O'er their heads, for the waves began to tremble
And the wall of flood to bend. Then arose
A cry of terror, baffled hate and hopeless dread,
A gurgling sound of horror, as "the waves
Came madly dashing, wildly crashing, seeking
Out their place again," and the flower and pride
Of Egypt sank as lead within the sea
Till the waves threw back their corpses cold and stark
Upon the shore, and the song of Israel's
Triumph was the requiem of their foes.
Oh the grandeur of that triumph; up the cliffs
And down the valleys, o'er the dark and restless

Sea, rose the people's shout of triumph, going
Up in praise to God, and the very air
Seemed joyous for the choral song of millions
Throbbed upon its viewless wings.
Then another song of triumph rose in accents
Soft and clear; 'twas the voice of Moses' sister
Rising in the tide of song. The warm blood
Of her childhood seemed dancing in her veins;
The roses of her girlhood were flushing
On her cheek, and her eyes flashed out the splendor
Of long departed days, for time itself seemed
Pausing, and she lived the past again; again
The Nile flowed by her; she was watching by the stream,
A little ark of rushes where her baby brother lay;
The tender tide of rapture swept o'er her soul again
She had felt when Pharaoh's daughter had claimed
Him as her own, and her mother wept for joy
Above her rescued son. Then again she saw
His choosing "twixt Israel's pain and sorrow
And Egypt's pomp and pride." But now he stood
Their leader triumphant on that shore, and loud
She struck the cymbals as she led the Hebrew women
In music, dance and song, as they shouted out
Triumphs in sweet and glad refrains.

MIRIAM'S SONG

A wail in the palace, a wail in the hut,
　　The midnight is shivering with dread,
And Egypt wakes up with a shriek and a sob
　　To mourn for her first-born and dead.

In the morning glad voices greeted the light,
　　As the Nile with splendor was flushed;
At midnight silence had melted their tones,
　　And their music forever is hushed.

In the morning the princes of palace and court
  To the heir of the kingdom bowed down;
'Tis midnight, pallid and stark in his shroud
  He dreams not of kingdom or crown.

As a monument blasted and blighted by God,
  Through the ages proud Pharaoh shall stand,
All seamed with the vengeance and scarred with the wrath
  That leaped from God's terrible hand.

Chapter VII

They journeyed on from Zuphim's sea until
They reached the sacred mount and heard the solemn
Decalogue. The mount was robed in blackness,—
Heavy and deep the shadows lay; the thunder
Crashed and roared upon the air: the lightning
Leaped from crag to crag; God's fearful splendor
Flowed around, and Sinai quaked and shuddered
To its base, and there did God proclaim
Unto their listening ears, the great, the grand,
The central and primal truth of all
The universe—the unity of God.
                  Only one God.—
This truth received into the world's great life,
Not as an idle dreamer's speculative thing,
But as a living, vitalizing thought,
Should bind us closer to our God and link us
With our fellow man, the brothers and co-heirs
With Christ, the elder brother of our race.
Before this truth let every blade of war
Grow dull, and slavery, cowering at the light,
Skulk from the homes of men; instead
Of war bring peace and freedom, love and joy,
And light for man, instead of bondage, whips
And chains. Only one God! the strongest hands

Should help the weak who bend before the blasts
Of life, because if God is only one
Then we are the children of his mighty hand,
And when we best serve man, we also serve
Our God. Let haughty rulers learn that men
Of humblest birth and lowliest lot have
Rights as sacred and divine as theirs, and they
Who fence in leagues of earth by bonds and claims
And title deeds, forgetting land and water,
Air and light are God's own gifts and heritage
For man—who throw their selfish lives between
God's sunshine and the shivering poor—
Have never learned the wondrous depth, nor scaled
The glorious height of this great central truth,
Around which clusters all the holiest faiths
Of earth. The thunder died upon the air,
The lightning ceased its livid play, the smoke
And darkness died away in clouds, as soft
And fair as summer wreaths that lie around
The setting sun, and Sinai stood a bare
And ragged thing among the sacred scenes
Of earth.

Chapter VIII

It was a weary thing to bear the burden
Of that restless and rebellious race. With
Sinai's thunders almost crashing in their ears,
They made a golden calf, and in the desert
Spread an idol's feast, and sung the merry songs
They had heard when Mizraim's songs bowed down before
Their vain and heathen gods; and thus for many years
Did Moses bear the evil manners of his race—
Their angry murmurs, fierce regrets and strange
Forgetfulness of God. Born slaves, they did not love

The freedom of the wild more than their pots of flesh.
And pleasant savory things once gathered
From the gardens of the Nile.
If Slavery only laid its weight of chains
Upon the weary, aching limbs, e'en then
It were a curse; but when it frets through nerve
And flesh and eats into the weary soul,
Oh then it is a thing for every human
Heart to loathe, and this was Israel's fate,
For when the chains were shaken from their limbs,
They failed to strike the impress from their souls.
While he who'd basked beneath the radiance
Of a throne, ne'er turned regretful eyes upon
The past, nor sighed to grasp again the pleasures
Once resigned; but the saddest trial was
To see the light and joy fade from their faces
When the faithless spies spread through their camp
Their ill report; and when the people wept
In hopeless unbelief and turned their faces
Egyptward, and asked a captain from their bands
To lead them back where they might bind anew
Their broken chains, when God arose and shut
The gates of promise on their lives, and left
Their bones to bleach beneath Arabia's desert sands
But though they slumbered in the wild, they died
With broader freedom on their lips, and for their
Little ones did God reserve the heritage
So rudely thrust aside.

THE DEATH OF MOSES
Chapter IX

His work was done; his blessing lay
Like precious ointment on his people's head,
And God's great peace was resting on his soul.

His life had been a lengthened sacrifice,
A thing of deep devotion to his race,
Since first he turned his eyes on Egypt's gild
And glow, and clasped their fortunes in his hand
And held them with a firm and constant grasp.
But now his work was done; his charge was laid
In Joshua's hand, and men of younger blood
Were destined to possess the land and pass
Through Jordan to the other side. He too
Had hoped to enter there—to tread the soil
Made sacred by the memories of his
Kindred dead, and rest till life's calm close beneath
The sheltering vines and stately palms of that
Fair land; that hope had colored all his life's
Young dreams and sent its mellowed flushes o'er
His later years; but God's decree was otherwise.
And so he bowed his meekened soul in calm
Submission to the word, which bade him climb
To Nebo's highest peak and view the pleasant land
From Jordan's swells unto the calmer ripples
Of the tideless sea, then die with all its
Loveliness in sight.
As he passed from Moab's grassy vale to climb
The rugged mount, the people stood in mournful groups,
Some, with quivering lips and tearful eyes,
Reaching out unconscious hands, as if to stay
His steps and keep him ever at their side, while
Others gazed with reverent awe upon
The calm and solemn beauty on his aged brow.
The look of loving trust and lofty faith
Still beaming from an eye that neither care
Nor time had dimmed. As he passed upward, tender
Blessings, earnest prayers and sad farewells rose
On each wave of air, then died in one sweet
Murmur of regretful love; and Moses stood
Alone on Nebo's mount.

Alone! not one
Of all that mighty throng who had trod with him
In triumph through the parted flood was there.
Aaron had died in Hor, with son and brother
By his side; and Miriam too was gone.
But kindred hands had made her grave, and Kadesh
Held her dust. But he was all alone; nor wife
Nor child was there to clasp in death his hand,
And bind around their bleeding hearts the precious
Parting words. And he was not all alone,
For God's great presence flowed around his path
And stayed him in that solemn hour.

He stood upon the highest peak of Nebo,
And saw the Jordan chafing through its gorges,
Its banks made bright by scarlet blooms
And purple blossoms. The placid lakes
And emerald meadows, the snowy crest
Of distant mountains, the ancient rocks
That dripped with honey, the hills all bathed
In light and beauty; the shady groves
And peaceful vistas, the vines opprest
With purple riches, the fig trees fruit-crowned
Green and golden, the pomegranates with crimson
Blushes, the olives with their darker clusters,
Rose before him like a vision, full of beauty
And delight. Gazed he on the lovely landscape
Till it faded from his view, and the wing
Of death's sweet angel hovered o'er the mountain's
Crest, and he heard his garments rustle through
The watches of the night.
                         Then another, fairer, vision
Broke upon his longing gaze; 'twas the land
Of crystal fountains, love and beauty, joy
And light, for the pearly gates flew open,
And his ransomed soul went in. And when morning

O'er the mountain fringed each crag and peak with light,
Cold and lifeless lay the leader. God had touched
His eyes with slumber, giving his beloved sleep.

Oh never on that mountain
Was seen a lovelier sight
Than the troupe of fair young angels
That gathered 'round the dead.
With gentle hands they bore him
That bright and shining train,
From Nebo's lonely mountain
To sleep in Moab's vale.
But they sang no mournful dirges,
No solemn requiems said,
And the soft wave of their pinions
Made music as they trod.
But no one heard them passing,
None saw their chosen grave;
It was the angels secret
Where Moses should be laid.
And when the grave was finished,
They trod with golden sandals
Above the sacred spot,
And the brightest, fairest flower
Sprang up beneath their tread.
Nor broken turf, nor hillock
Did e'er reveal that grave,
And truthful lips have never said
We know where he is laid.

THE RAGGED STOCKING

Do you see this ragged stocking,
    Here a rent and there a hole?
Each thread of this little stocking
    Is woven around my soul.

Do you wish to hear my story?
    Excuse me, the tears will start,
For the sight of this ragged stocking
    Stirs the fountains of my heart.

You say that my home is happy;
    To me 'tis earth's fairest place,
But its sunshine, peace and gladness
    Back to this stocking I trace.

I was once a wretched drunkard;
    Ah! you start and say not so;
But the dreadful depths I've sounded,
    And I speak of what I know.

I was wild and very reckless
    When I stood on manhood's brink,
And joining with pleasure-seekers
    Learned to revel and drink.

Strong drink is a raging demon,
    In his hands are shame and woe,
He mocketh the strength of the mighty
    And bringeth the strong man low.

The light of my home was darkened
    By the shadow of my sin;
And want and woe unbarr'd the door,
    And suffering entered in.

The streets were full one Christmas eve,
   And alive with girls and boys,
Merrily looking through window-panes
   At bright and beautiful toys.

And throngs of parents came to buy
   The gifts that children prize,
And homeward trudged with happy hearts,
   The love-light in their eyes.

I thought of my little Charley
   At home in his lowly bed,
With the shadows around his life,
   And in shame I bowed my head.

I entered my home a sober man,
   My heart by remorse was wrung,
And there in the chimney corner,
   This little stocking was hung.

Faded and worn as you see it;
   To me 'tis a precious thing,
And I never gaze upon it
   But unbidden tears will spring.

I began to search my pockets,
   But scarcely a dime was there;
But scanty as was the pittance,
   This stocking received its share.

For a longing seized upon me
   To gladden the heart of my boy,
And I brought him some cakes and candy,
   And added a simple toy.

Then I knelt by this little stocking
   And sobbed out an earnest prayer,
And arose with strength to wrestle
   And break from the tempter's snare.

And this faded, worn-out stocking,
  So pitiful once to see,
Became the wedge that broke my chain,
  And a blessing brought to me.

Do you marvel then I prize it?
  When each darn and seam and hole
Is linked with my soul's deliverance
  From the bondage of the bowl?

And to-night my wife will tell you,
  Though I've houses, gold and land,
He holds no treasure more precious
  Than this stocking in my hand.

THE FATAL PLEDGE

"Pledge me with wine," the maiden cried,
  Her tones were gay and light;
"From others you have turned aside,
  I claim your pledge to-night."

The blood rushed to the young man's cheek,
  Then left it deadly pale;
Beneath the witchery of her smile
  He felt his courage fail.

For many years he'd been a slave
  To the enchanting bowl,
Until he grasped with eager hands
  The reins of self-control;

And struggled with his hated thrall,
  Until he rent his chain,
And strove to stand erect and free,
  And be a man again.

When others came with tempting words
   He coldly turned aside,
But she who held the sparkling cup
   Was his affianced bride;

And like a vision of delight,
   Bright, beautiful and fair,
With thoughtless words she wove for him
   The meshes of despair.

With jeweled hands he took the cup,
   Nor heard the serpent's hiss;
Nor saw beneath the ruby glow
   The deadly adder's hiss.

Like waves that madly, wildly dash,
   When dykes are overthrown,
The barriers of his soul gave way,
   Each life with wrecks was strewn.

And she who might have reached her hand
   To succor and to save,
Soon wept in hopeless agony
   Above a drunkard's grave.

And bore through life a bleeding heart
   Remembrance of that night,
When she had urged the tempted man
   With wine to make his plight.

CHRIST'S ENTRY INTO JERUSALEM

He had plunged into our sorrows,
   And our sin had pierced his heart,
As before him loomed death's shadow,
   And he knew he must depart.

But they hailed him as a victor
  As he into Salem came,
And the very children shouted
  Loud hosannas to his name.

But he knew behind that triumph,
  Rising gladly to the sky,
Soon would come the cries of malice:
  Crucify him! Crucify!

Onward rode the blessed Saviour,
  Conscious of the coming strife
Soon to break in storms of hatred
  Round his dear, devoted life.

Ghastly in its fearful anguish
  Rose the cross before his eyes,
But he saw the joy beyond it,
  And did all the shame despise.

Joy to see the cry of scorning
  Through the ages ever bright,
In the cross of shame transfigured
  To a throne of love and light.

Joy to know his soul's deep travail
  Should not be a thing in vain,
And that joy and peace should blossom
  From his agonizing pain.

THE RESURRECTION OF JESUS

It was done, the deed of horror;
  Christ had died upon the cross,
And within an upper chamber
  The disciples mourned their loss.

Peter's eyes were full of anguish,
  Thinking sadly of the trial
When his boasted self-reliance
  Ended in his Lord's denial.

Disappointment, deep and heavy,
  Shrouded every heart with gloom,
As the hopes so fondly cherished
  Died around the garden tomb.

And they thought with shame and sorrow
  How they fled in that dark hour,
When they saw their Lord and Master
  In the clutch of Roman power.

We had hoped, they sadly uttered,
  He would over Israel reign,
But to-day he lies sepulchred,
  And our cherished hopes are vain.

In the humble home of Mary
  Slowly waned the hours away,
Till she rose to seek the garden
  And the place where Jesus lay.

Not the cross with all its anguish
  Could her loving heart restrain,
But the tomb she sought was empty,
  And her heart o'erflowed with pain.

To embalm my Lord and Master
  To this garden I have strayed,
But, behold, I miss his body,
  And I know not where he's laid.

Then a wave of strange emotion
  Swept her soul, as angels said,
"Wherefore do ye seek the living
  'Mid the chambers of the dead?"

Unperceived, her Lord stood by her,
   Silent witness of her grief,
Bearing on his lips the tidings
   Sure to bring a glad relief.

But her tear-dimmed eyes were holden
   Then she heard the Master speak;
Thought she, only 'tis the gardener
   Asking whom her soul did seek.

Then a sudden flush of gladness
   O'er her grief-worn features spread;
When she knew the voice of Jesus
   All her bitter anguish fled.

Forth she reached hands in rapture.
   "Touch me not," the Saviour said;
"Take the message to my brethren,
   I have risen from the dead.

"Take them words of joy and comfort,
   Which will all their mourning end;
To their father and my father,
   Tell them that I will ascend."

"Brethren, I have seen the Master:
   He is risen from the dead."
But like words of idle meaning
   Seemed the glorious words she said.

Soon they saw the revelation
   Which would bid their mourning cease:
Christ, the risen, stood before them
   Breathing words of love and peace.

Timid men were changed to heroes,
   Weakness turned to wondrous might,
And the cross became their standard,
   Luminous with love and light.

From that lonely upper chamber,
   Holding up the rugged cross,
With a glad and bold surrender
   They encountered shame and loss.

In these days of doubt and error,
   In the conflict for the right,
May our hearts be ever strengthened
   By the resurrection's might.

SIMON'S COUNTRYMEN

They took away his seamless robe,
   With thorns they crowned his head,
As harshly, fiercely cried his foes:
   "Barabbas in his stead."

The friends he loved unto the end,
   Who shared his daily bread,
Before the storms of wrath and hate
   Forsook their Lord and fled.

To rescue men from death and sin
   He knew the awful cost,
As wearily he bent beneath
   The burden of the cross.

When Pilate had declared his fate,
   And Jews withheld their aid,
Then Simon, the Cyrenean, came:
   On him the cross was laid.

Not his to smite with cruel scorn,
   Nor mock the dying one,
That helpful man came from the land
   Missed by the ardent sun—

The land within whose sheltering arms
   The infant Jesus lay
When Herod vainly bared his sword
   And sought the child to slay.

Amid the calendar of saints
   We Simon's name may trace,
On history's page thro' every age
   He bears an honored place.

He little knew that cross would change
   Unto a throne of light;
The crown of thorns upon Christ's brow
   Would be forever bright.

Beneath the shadow of that cross
   Brave men with outstretched hands
Have told the wondrous tale of love
   In distant heathen lands.

And yet within our favored land,
   Where Christian churches rise,
The dark-browed sons of Africa
   Are hated and despised.

Can they who speak of Christ as King,
   And glory in his name,
Forget that Simon's countrymen
   Still bear a cross of shame?

Can they forget the cruel scorn
   Men shower on a race
Who treat the hues their father gives
   As emblems of disgrace?

Will they erect to God their fanes
   And Christ with honor crown,
And then with cruel weights of pain
   The African press down?

Oh, Christians, when we faint and bleed
　　In this our native land,
Reach out to us when peeled, opprest,
　　A kindly helping hand,

And bear aloft that sacred cross,
　　Bright from the distant years,
And say for Christ's and Simon's sake,
　　We'll wipe away your tears.

For years of sorrow, toil and pain
　　We'll bring you love and light,
And in the name of Christ our Lord
　　We'll make your pathway bright.

That seamless robe shall yet enfold
　　The children of the sun,
Till rich and poor and bond and free
　　In Christ shall all be one.

And for his sake from pride and scorn
　　Our spirits shall be free,
Till through our souls shall sound the words
　　He did it unto me.

DELIVERANCE

Rise up! rise up! Oh Israel,
　　Let a spotless lamb be slain;
The angel of death will o'er you bend
　　And rend your galling chain.

Sprinkle its blood upon the posts
　　And lintels of your door;
When the angel sees the crimson spots
　　Unharmed he will pass you o'er.

Gather your flocks and herds to-night,
   Your children by your side;
A leader from Arabia comes
   To be your friend and your guide.

With girded loins and sandled feet
   Await the hour of dread,
When Mizraim shall wildly mourn
   Her first-born and her dead.

The sons of Abraham no more
   Shall crouch 'neath Pharaoh's hand,
Trembling with agony and dread.
   He'll thrust you from the land.

And ye shall hold in unborn years
   A feast to mark this day,
When joyfully the fathers rose
   And cast their chains away.

When crimson tints of morning flush
   The golden gates of day,
Or gorgeous hue of even melt
   In sombre shades away,

Then ye shall to your children teach
   The meaning of this feast,
How from the proud oppressor's hand
   Their fathers were released,

And ye shall hold through distant years
   This feast with glad accord,
And children's children yet shall learn
   To love and trust the Lord.

Ages have passed since Israel trod
   In triumph through the sea,
And yet they hold in memory's urn
   Their first great jubilee,

When Moses led the ransomed hosts,
    And Miriam's song arose,
While ruin closed around the path
    Of their pursuing foes.

Shall Israel thro' long varied years
    These memories cherish yet,
And we who lately stood redeemed
    Our broken chains forget?

Should we forget the wondrous change
    That to our people came,
When justice rose and sternly plead
    Our cause with sword and flame,

And led us through the storms of war
    To freedom's fairer shore,
When slavery sank beneath a flood
    Whose waves were human gore?

Oh, youth and maidens of the land,
    Rise up with one accord,
And in the names of Christ go forth
    To battle for the Lord.

Go forth, but not in crimson fields,
    With fratricidal strife,
But in the name of Christ go forth
    For freedom, love and life.

Go forth to follow in his steps,
    Who came not to destroy,
Till wasteds shall blossom as the rose,
    And deserts sing for joy.

SIMON'S FEAST

He is coming, she said, to Simon's feast,
   The prophet of Galilee,
Though multitudes around him throng
   In longing his face to see.

He enters the home as Simon's guest,
   But he gives no welcome kiss;
He brings no water to bathe his feet—
   Why is Simon so remiss?

If a prophet, he will surely know
   The guilt of my darkened years;
With broken heart I'll see his face,
   And bathe his feet with my tears.

No holy rabbi lays his hand
   In blessing on my head;
No loving voice floats o'er the path,
   The downer path I tread.

Unto the Master's side she pressed,
   A penitent, rail and fair,
Rained on his feet a flood of tears,
   And then wiped them with her hair.

Over the face of Simon swept
   An air of puzzled surprise;
Can my guest a holy prophet be,
   And not this woman despise?

Christ saw the thoughts that Simon's heart
   Had written upon his face,
Kindly turned to the sinful one
   In her sorrow and disgrace.

Where Simon only saw the stains,
    Where sin and shame were rife,
Christ looked beneath and saw the perms
    Or a fair, outflowering life.

Like one who breaks a galling chain,
    And sets a prisoner free,
He rent her fetters with the words,
    "Thy sins are forgiven thee."

God be praised for the gracious words
    Which came through that woman's touch,
That souls redeemed thro' God's dear Son
    May learn to love him so much;

That souls once red with guilt and crime
    May their crimson stains outgrow;
The scarlet spots upon their lives
    Become whiter than driven snow.

LINES TO HON. THADDEUS STEVENS

Have the bright and glowing visions
    Faded from thy longing sight,
Like the gorgeous tints of ev'n
    Mingling with the shades of night?

Didst thou hope to see thy country
    Wearing Justice as a crown,
Standing foremost 'mid the nations
    Worthy of the world's renown?

Didst thou think the grand fruition
    Reached the fullness of its time,
When the crater of God's judgment
    Overflowed the nation's crime?

That thy people, purged by fire,
  Would have trod another path,
Careful, lest their feet should stumble
  On the cinders of God's wrath?

And again the injured negro
  Grind the dreadful mills of fate,
Pressing out the fearful vintage
  Of the nation's scorn and hate?

Sadder than the crimson shadows
  Hung for years around our skies,
Are the hopes so fondly cherished
  Fading now before thine eyes.

Not in vain has been thy hoping,
  Though thy fair ideals fade,
If, like one of God's tall aloes,
  Thou art rip'ning in the shade.

There is light beyond the darkness,
  Joy beyond the present pain;
There is hope in God's great justice,
  And the negro's rising brain.

Though before the timid counsels
  Truth and Right may seem to fail.
God hath bathed his sword in judgment,
  And his arm shall yet prevail.

AN APPEAL TO
THE AMERICAN PEOPLE

When a dark and fearful strife
Raged around the nation's life,
And the traitor plunged his steel

Where your quivering hearts could feel,
When your cause did need a friend,
We were faithful to the end.

When we stood with bated breath,
Facing fiery storms of death,
And the war-cloud, red with wrath,
Fiercely swept around our path,
Did our hearts with terror quail?
Or our courage ever fail?

When the captive, wanting bread,
Sought our poor and lowly shed,
And the blood-hounds missed his way,
Did we e'er his path betray?
Filled we not his heart with trust
As we shared with him our crust?

With your soldiers, side by side,
helped we turn the battle's tide,
Till o'er ocean, stream and shore,
Waved the rebel flag no more,
And above the rescued sod
Praises rose to freedom's God.

But to-day the traitor stands
With crimson on his hands,
Scowling 'neath his brow of hate,
On our weak and desolate,
With the blood-rust on the knife
Aimed at the nation's life.

Asking you to weakly yield
All we won upon the field,
To ignore, on land and flood,
All the offerings of our blood,
And to write above our slain
"They have fought and died in vain."

To your manhood we appeal,
Lest the traitor's iron heel
Grind and trample in the dust
All our new-born hope and trust,
And the name of freedom be
Linked with bitter mockery.

TRUTH

A rock, for ages, stern and high,
Stood frowning 'gainst the earth and sky,
And never bowed his haughty crest
With angry storms around him prest.
Morn, springing from the arms of night,
Had often bathed his brow with light,
And kissed the shadows from his face
With tender love and gentle grace.

Day, pausing at the gates of rest,
Smiled on him from the distant West,
And from her throne the dark-browed Night
Threw round his path her softest light.
And yet he stood unmoved and proud,
Nor love, nor wrath, his spirit bowed;
He bared his brow to every blast
And scorned the tempest as it passed.

One day a tiny, humble seed—
The keenest eye would hardly heed—
Fell trembling at that stern rock's base,
And found a lowly hiding-place.
A ray of light, and drop of dew,
Came with a message, kind and true;
They told her of the world so bright,
Its love, its joy, and rosy light,

And lured her from her hiding-place,
To gaze upon earth's glorious face.

So, peeping timid from the ground,
She clasped the ancient rock around,
And climbing up with childish grace,
She held him with a close embrace;
Her clinging was a thing of dread;
Wher'er she touched a fissure spread,
And he who'd breasted many a storm
Stood frowning there, a mangled form;
A Truth, dropped in the silent earth,
May seem a thing of little worth,
Till, spreading round some mighty wrong,
It saps its pillars proud and strong,
And o'er the fallen ruin weaves
The brightest blooms and fairest leaves.

DEATH OF THE OLD SEA KING

'Twas a fearful night—the tempest raved
    With loud and wrathful pride
The storm-king harnessed his lightning steeds
    And rode on the raging tide.

The sea-king lay on his bed of death,
    Pale mourners around him bent;
They knew the wild and fitful life
    Of their chief was almost spent.

His ear was growing dull in death
    When the angry storm he heard,
The sluggish blood in the old man's veins
    With sudden vigor stirred.

"I hear them call," cried the dying man,
    His eyes grew full of light;

"Now bring me here my warrior robes,
 My sword and armor bright.

"In the tempest's lull I heard a voice,
 I knew 'twas Odin's call.
The Valkyrs are gathering round my bed
 To lead me unto his hall.

"Bear me unto my noblest ship,
 Light up a funeral pyre;
I'll walk to the palace of the braves
 Through a path of flame and fire."

Oh! wild and bright was the stormy light
 That flashed from the old man's eye,
As they bore him from the couch of death
 To his battle-ship to die,

And lit with many a mournful torch
 The sea-king's dying bed,
And like a banner fair and bright
 The flames around him spread.

But they heard no cry of anguish
 Break through that fiery wall,
With rigid brow and silent lips
 He was seeking Odin's hall.

Through a path of fearful splendor,
 While strong men held their breath,
The brave old man went boldly forth
 And calmly talked with death.

LET THE LIGHT ENTER!
The dying words of Goethe

"Light! more light! the shadows deepen,
 And my life is ebbing low,

Throw the windows widely open;
    Light! more light! before I go.

"Softly let the balmy sunshine
    Play around my dying bed,
O'er the dimly lighted valley
    I with lonely feet must tread.

"Light! more light! for Death is weaving
    Shadows 'round my waning sight,
And I fain would gaze upon him
    Through a stream of earthly light."

Not for greater gifts of genius;
    Not for thoughts more grandly bright.
All the dying poet whispers
    Is a prayer for light, more light.

Heeds he not the gathered laurels,
    Fading slowly from his sight;
All the poet's aspirations
    Centre in that prayer for light.

Gracious Saviour, when life's day-dreams
    Melt and vanish from the sight,
May our dim and longing vision
    Then be blessed with light, more light.

YOUTH IN HEAVEN

"In heaven, the angels are advancing continually to the
spring-time of their youth, so that the oldest angel appears
the youngest."

SWEDENBORG

Not for them the length'ning shadows,
    Fallingly coldly 'round our lives;

Nearer, nearer, through the ages,
　　Life's new spring for them arrives.

Not for them the doubt and anguish
　　Of an old and loveless age;
Dropping sadly tears of sorrow,
　　On life's faded, blotted, page.

Not for them the hopeless clinging,
　　To life's worn and feeble strands;
Till the last has ceased to tremble,
　　In our aged, withered hands.

Not for them the mournful dimming
　　Of the weary tear-stained eye,
That has seen the sad procession,
　　Of its dearest hopes go by.

Never lines of light and darkness
　　Thread the brows forever fair;
And the eldest of the angels,
　　Seems the youngest brother there.

There the streets of life doth never
　　Cross the mournful plain of death;
And the gates of light are ever
　　Closed against its icy breath.

DEATH OF ZOMBI
The Chief of a Negro Kingdom
in South Africa

Cruel in vengeance, reckless in wrath,
The hunters of men bore down on our path;
Inhuman and fierce, the offer they gave
Was freedom in death or the life of a slave.
The cheek of the mother grew pallid with dread,

As the tidings of evil around us were spread,
And closer and closer she strained to her heart
The children she feared they would sever apart.
The brows of our maidens grew gloomy and sad;
Hot tears burst from eyes once sparkling and glad.
Our young men stood ready to join in the fray,
That hung as a pall 'round our people that day.
Our leaders gazed angry and stern on the strife,
For freedom to them was dearer than life.
There was mourning at home and death in the street,
For carnage and famine together did meet.
The pale lips of hunger were asking for bread,
While husbands and fathers lay bleeding and dead.
For days we withstood the tempests of wrath,
That scattered destruction and death in our path,
Till, broken and peeled, we yielded at last,
And the glory and strength of our kingdom were past.
But Zombi, our leader, and warlike old chief,
Gazed down on our woe with anger and grief;
The tyrant for him forged fetters in vain,
His freedom-girt limbs had worn their last chain.
A freeman he'd lived and free he would die.
Defiance and daring still flashed from his eye;
So he climbed to the verge of a dangerous steep,
Resolved from its margin to take a last leap;
For a fearful death and a bloody grave
Were dearer to him than the life of a slave.
Nor went he alone to the mystic land—
There were other warriors in his band,
Who rushed with him to Death's dark gate,
All wrapped in the shroud of a mournful fate.

LINES TO CHARLES SUMNER

Thank God that thou hast spoken
  Words earnest, true and brave,
The lightning of thy lips did smite
  The fetters of the slave.

I thought the shadows deepened,
  Round the pathway of the slave,
As one by one his faithful friends
  Were dropping in the grave.

When other hands grew feeble,
  And loosed their hold on life,
Thy words rang like a clarion
  For freedom's noble strife.

Thy words were not soft echoes,
  Thy tones no syren song;
They fell as battle-axes
  upon our giant wrong.

God grant thy words of power
  May fall as precious seeds,
That yet shall leaf and blossom
  In high and holy deeds.

"SIR, WE WOULD SEE JESUS"

We would see Jesus; earth is grand,
Glowing out from her Creator's hand.
Like one who tracks his steps with light,
His footsteps ever greet our sight;
The earth below, the sky above,
Are full of tokens of his love;

But 'mid the fairest scenes we've sighed—
Our hearts are still unsatisfied.

We would see Jesus; proud and high
Temples and domes have met our eye.
We've gazed upon the glorious thought,
By earnest hands in marble wrought,
And listened where the flying feet
Beat time to music, soft and sweet;
But bow'rs of ease, and halls of pride,
Our yearning hearts ne'er satisfied.

We would see Jesus; we have heard
Tidings our inmost souls have stirred,
How, from their chambers full of night,
The darkened eyes receive the light;
How, at the music of his voice,
The lame do leap, the dumb rejoice.
Anxious we'll wait until we've seen
The good and gracious Nazarene.

THE BRIDE OF DEATH

They robed her for another groom,
For her bridal couch, prepared the tomb;
From the sunny love of her marriage day
A stronger rival had won her away;
His wooing was like a stern command,
And cold was the pressure of his hand.

Through her veins he sent an icy thrill,
With sudden fear her heart stood still;
To his dusty palace the bride he led,
Her guests were the pale and silent dead.

No eye flashed forth a loving light,
To greet the bride as she came in sight,
Not one reached out a joyous hand,
To welcome her home to the mystic land.

Silent she sat in the death still hall,
For her bridal robe she wore a pall;
Instead of orange-blossoms fair,
Willow and cypress wreathed her hair.
Though her mother's kiss lay on her cheek,
Her lips no answering love could speak,
No air of life stirred in her breath,
That fair young girl was the bride of death.

THANK GOD FOR LITTLE CHILDREN

Thank God for little children;
    Bright flowers by earth's wayside,
The dancing, joyous lifeboats
    Upon life's stormy tide.

Thank God for little children;
    When our skies are cold and gray,
They come as sunshine to our hearts,
    And charm our cares away.

I almost think the angels,
    Who tend life's garden fair,
Drop down the sweet wild blossoms
    That bloom around us here.

It seems a breath of heaven
    Round many a cradle lies,
And every little baby
    Brings a message from the skies.

Dear mothers, guard these jewels,
  As sacred offerings meet,
A wealth of household treasures
  To lay at Jesus' feet.

THE DYING FUGITIVE

Slowly o'er his darkened features,
Stole the warning shades of death;
And we knew the shadowing angel
Waited for his parting breath.

He had started for his freedom;
And his heart beat firm and high—
But before he won the guerdon,
Came the message—he must die.

He must die, when just before him,
Lay the longed for, precious prize—
And the hopes that lit him onward,
Faded out before his eyes.

For a while a fearful madness,
Rested on his weary brain;
And he thought the hateful tyrant,
Had rebound his galling chain.

Then he raved in bitter anguish—
"Take me where that good man dwells!"
To a name to freedom precious;—
Lingered mid life's shattered cells.

But as sunshine gently stealing,
O'er the storm-cloud's gloomy track—
Through the tempests of his bosom,
Came the light of reason back.

And without a sigh or murmur
For the home he'd left behind;
Calmly yielded he his spirit,
To the father of mankind.

Thankful that so near to freedom,
He with eager steps had trod—
E'er his ransomed spirit rested,
On the bosom of his God.

BURY ME IN A FREE LAND

Make me a grave where'er you will,
In a lowly plain, or a lofty hill,
Make it among earth's humblest graves,
But not in a land where men are slaves.

I could not rest if around my grave
I heard the steps of a trembling slave:
His shadow above my silent tomb
Would make it a place of fearful gloom.

I could not rest if I heard the tread
Of a coffle gang to the shambles led,
And the mother's shriek of wild despair
Rise like a curse on the trembling air.

I could not sleep if I saw the lash
Drinking her blood at each fearful gash,
And I saw her babes torn from her breast,
Like trembling doves from their parent nest.

I'd shudder and start if I heard the bay
Of blood-hounds seizing their human prey,
And I heard the captive plead in vain
As they bound afresh his galling chain.

If I saw young girls from their mother's arms
Bartered and sold for their youthful charms,
My eye would flash with a mournful flame,
My death-paled cheek grow red with shame.

I would sleep, dear friends, where bloated might
Can rob no man of his dearest right;
My rest shall be calm in any grave
Where none can call his brother a slave.

I ask no monument, proud and high
To arrest the gaze of the passers-by;
All that my yearning spirit craves,
Is bury me not in a land of slaves.

THE FREEDOM BELL

Ring, aye, ring the freedom bell,
 And let its tones be loud and clear;
With glad hosannas let it swell
 Until it reach the Bondman's ear.

Through pain that wrings the life apart,
 And spasms full of deadly strife,
And throes that shake the nation's heart,
 The fainting land renews her life.

Where shrieks and groans distract the air,
 And sods grow red with crimson rain,
The ransom'd slave shall kneel in prayer
 And bury deep his rusty chain.

There cheeks now pale with sickening dread,
 And brows grow dark with cruel wrath,
Shall Freedom's banner wide be spread
 And Hope and Peace attend her path.

White-robed and pure her feet shall move
   O'er rifts of ruin deep and wide;
Her hands shall span with lasting love
   The chasms rent by hate and pride.

There waters, blush'd with human gore,
   Unsullied streams shall purl along;
Where crashed the battle's awful roar
   Shall rise the Freeman's joyful song.

Then ring, aye, ring the freedom bell,
   Proclaiming all the nation free;
Let earth with sweet thanksgiving swell
   And heaven catch up the melody.

MARY AT THE FEET
OF CHRIST

She stood at Jesus' feet,
   And bathed them with her tears,
While o'er her spirit surg'd
   The guilt and shame of years.

Though Simon saw the grief
   Upon the fair young face,
The stern man coldly thought
   For her this is no place.

Her feet have turned aside
   From paths of truth and right,
If Christ a prophet be
   He'll spurn her from his sight.

And silently he watched
   The child of sin and care,

Uncoil upon Christ's feet
　　Her wealth of raven hair.

O Life! she sadly thought,
　　I know thy bane and blight,
And yet I fain would find
　　The path of peace and right.

I've seen the leper cleansed,
　　I've seen the sick made whole,
But mine's a deeper wound—
　　It eats into the soul.

And men have trampled down
　　The beauty once their prize,
While women pass me by
　　With cold, averted eyes.

But now a hope of peace
　　Steals o'er my weary breast,
And from these lips of love
　　There comes a sense of rest.

The tender, loving Christ
　　Gazed on her tearful eyes,
Then saw on Simon's face
　　A look of cold surprise.

"Simon," the Saviour said,
　　"Thou wast to me remiss,
I came thy guest, but thou
　　Didst give no welcome kiss.

"Thou broughtest from thy fount
　　No water cool and sweet,
But she, with many tears,
　　Hath bent and kissed my feet.

"Thou pouredst on my head
　　No oil with kindly care,
But she anoints my feet,
　　And wipes them with her hair.

"I know her steps have strayed,
　　Her sins they many be,
But she with love hath bound
　　Her erring heart to me."

How sweetly fell his words
　　Upon her bruised heart,
When, like a ghastly train,
　　She felt her sins depart.

What music heard on earth,
　　Or rapture moving heaven
Were like those precious words—
　　"Thy sins were all forgiven!"

THE MOTHER'S BLESSING

Oh, my soul had grown so weary
　　With its many cares opprest,
All my heart's high aspiration
　　Languish'd in a prayer for rest.

I was like a lonely stranger
　　Pining in a distant land,
Bearing on her lips a language
　　None around her understand.

Longing for close communion
　　With some kindred mind and heart,
But whose language is a jargon
　　Past her skill, and past her art.

God in mercy looked upon me,
    Saw my fainting, pain and strife,
Sent to me a blest evangel,
    Through the gates of light and life.

Then my desert leafed and blossom'd,
    Beauty decked its deepest wild,
Hope and joy, peace and blessing,
    Met me in my first-born child.

When the tiny hands, so feeble,
    Brought me smiles and joyful tears,
Lifted from my life the shadows,
    That had gathered there for years.

God, I thank thee for the blessing
    That at last has crown'd my life,
Soothed its weary, lonely anguish,
    Stayed its fainting, calm'd its strife.

Gracious Parent! guard and shelter
    In thine arms my darling child
Till she treads the streets of jasper,
    Glorified and undefiled.

VASHTI

She leaned her head upon her hand
    And heard the the King's decree—
"My lords are feasting in my halls;
    Bid Vashti come to me.

"I've shown the treasures of my house,
    My costly jewels rare,
But with the glory of her eyes
    No rubies can compare.

"Adorn'd and crown'd I'd have her come,
    With all her queenly grace,
And, 'mid my lords and mighty men,
    Unveil her lovely face.

"Each gem that sparkles in my crown,
    Or glitters on my throne,
Grows poor and pale when she appears,
    My beautiful, my own!"

All waiting stood the chamberlains
    To hear the Queen's reply.
They saw her cheek grow deathly pale,
    But light flash'd to her eye:

"Go, tell the King," she proudly said,
    "That I am Persia's Queen,
And by his crowds of merry men
    I never will be seen.

"I'll take the crown from off my head
    And tread it 'neath my feet,
Before their rude and careless gaze
    My shrinking eyes shall meet.

"A queen unveil'd before the crowd!—
    Upon each lip my name!—
Why, Persia's women all would blush
    And weep for Vashti's shame!

"Go back!" she cried, and waved her hand,
    And grief was in her eye:
"Go, tell the King," she sadly said,
    "That I would rather die."

They brought her message to the King;
    Dark flash'd his angry eye;
'Twas as the lightning ere the storm
    Hath swept in fury by.

Then bitterly outspoke the King,
    Through purple lips of wrath—
"What shall be done to her who dares
    To cross your monarch's path?"

Then spoke his wily counsellors—
    "O King of this fair land!
From distant Ind to Ethiop,
    All bow to thy command.

"But if, before thy servant's eyes,
    This thing they plainly see,
That Vashti doth not heed thy will
    Nor yield herself to thee,

"The women, restive 'neath our rule,
    Would learn to scorn our name,
And from her deed to us would come
    Reproach and burning shame.

"Then, gracious King, sign with thy hand
    This stern but just decree,
That Vashti lay aside her crown,
    Thy Queen no more to be."

She heard again the King's command,
    And left her high estate;
Strong in her earnest womanhood,
    She calmly met her fate.

And left the palace of the King,
    Proud of her spotless name—
A woman who could bend to grief,
    But would not bow to shame.

THE CHANGE

The blue sky arching overhead,
The green turf 'neath my daily tread,
All glorified by freedom's light,
Grow fair and lovely to my sight.

The very winds that sweep along
Seemed burdened with a lovely song,
Nor shrieks nor groans of grief or fear,
Float on their wings and pain my ear.

No more with dull and aching breast,
Roused by the horn—I rise from rest.
Content and cheerful with my lot,
I greet the sun and leave my cot.

For darling child and loving wife
I toil with newly waken'd life;
The light that lingers round her smile
The shadows from my soul beguile.

The prattle of my darling boy
Fills my old heart with untold joy;
Before his laughter, mirth and song
Fade out long scores of grief and wrong.

Oh, never did the world appear
So lovely to my eye and ear,
'Till Freedom came, with Joy and Peace,
And bade my hateful bondage cease!

THE DYING MOTHER

Come nearer to me, husband
  Now the aching leaves my breast,

But my eyes are dim and weary,
    And to-night I fain would rest.

Clasp me closer to your bosom
    Ere I calmly sleep in death;
With your arms enfolded round me
    I would yield my parting breath.

Bring me now my darling baby,
    God's own precious gift of love,
Tell her she must meet her mother
    In the brighter world above.

When her little feet grow stronger
    To walk life's paths untrod,
That earnest, true and hopeful,
    She must lay her hands on God.

Tell my other little children
    They must early seek His face;
That His love is a strong tower,
    And His arms a hiding place.

Tell them—but my voice grows fainter—
    Surely, husband, this is death—
Tell them that their dying mother
    Bless'd them with her latest breath.

WORDS FOR THE HOUR

Men of the North! it is no time
    To quit the battle-field;
When danger fronts your rear and van
    It is no time to yield.

No time to bend the battle's crest
   Before the wily foe,
And, ostrich-like, to hide your heads
   From the impending blow.

The minions of a baffled wrong
   Are marshalling their clan,
Rise up, rise up, enchanted North!
   And strike for God and man.

This is no time for careless ease;
   No time for idle sleep;
Go light the fires in every camp,
   And solemn sentries keep.

The foe ye foiled upon the field
   Has only changed his base;
New dangers crowd around you
   And stare you in the face.

O Northern men! within your hands
   Is held no common trust;
Secure the victories won by blood
   When treason bit the dust.

'Tis yours to banish from the land
   Oppression's iron rule;
And o'er the ruin'd auction-block
   Erect the common school.

To wipe from labor's branded brow
   The curse that shames the land;
And teach the freedman how to wield
   The ballot in his hand.

This is the nation's golden hour,
   Nerve every heart and hand,
To build on Justice, as a rock,
   The future of the land.

True to your trust, oh, never yield
   One citadel of right!
With Truth and Justice clasping hands
   Ye yet shall win the fight!

PRESIDENT LINCOLN'S PROCLAMATION OF FREEDOM

It shall flash through the coming ages;
   It shall light the distant years;
And eyes now dim with sorrow
   Shall be clearer through their tears.

It shall flush the mountain ranges;
   And the valleys shall grow bright;
It shall bathe the hills in radiance,
   And crown their brows with light.

It shall flood with golden splendor
   And the huts of Caroline,
And the sun-kissed brow of labor
   With lustre new shall shine.

It shall gild the gloomy prison,
   Darken'd by the nation's crime,
Where the dumb and patient millions
   Wait the better coming time.

By the light that gilds their prison,
   They shall seize its mould'ring key,
And the bolts and bars shall vibrate
   With the triumphs of the free.

Like the dim and ancient chaos,
   Shrinking from the dawn of light,
Oppression, grim and hoary,
   Shall cower at the sight.

And her spawn of lies and malice
   Shall grovel in the dust,
While joy shall thrill the bosoms
   Of the merciful and just.

Though the morning seemed to linger
   O'er the hill-tops far away,
Now the shadows bear the promise
   Of the quickly coming day.

Soon the mists and murky shadows
   Shall be fringed with crimson light,
And the glorious dawn of freedom
   Break refulgent on the sight.

TO A BABE SMILING
IN HER SLEEP

Tell me, did the angels greet thee?
   Greet my darling when she smiled?
Did they whisper, softly, gently,
   Pleasant thoughts unto my child?

Did they whisper, 'mid thy dreaming,
   Thoughts that made thy spirit glad?
Of the joy-lighted city,
   Where the heart is never sad?

Did they tell thee of the fountains,
   Clear as crystal, fair as light,
And the glory-brightened country,
   Never shaded by a night?

Of life's pure, pellucid river,
   And the tree whose leaves do yield
Healing for the wounded nations—
   Nations smitten, bruised and peeled?

Of the city, ruby-founded,
    Built on gems of flashing light,
Paling all earth's lustrous jewels,
    And the gates of pearly white?

Darling, when life's shadows deepen
    Round thy prison-house of clay,
May the footsteps of God's angels
    Ever linger round thy way.

THE ARTIST

He stood before his finished work;
    His heart beat warm and high;
But they who gazed upon the youth
    Knew well that he must die.

For many days a fever fierce
    Had burned into his life;
But full of high impassioned art,
    He bore the fearful strife.

And wrought in extacy and hope
    The image of his brain;
He felt the death throes at his heart,
    But labored through the pain.

The statue seemed to glow with life—
    A costly work of art;
For it he paid the fervent blood
    From his own eager heart.

With kindling eye and flushing cheek
    But slowly laboring breath,
He gazed upon his finished work,
    Then sought his couch of death.

And when the plaudits of the crowd
  Came like the south wind's breath,
The dreamy, gifted child of art
  Had closed his eyes in death.

JESUS

Come speak to me of Jesus,
  I love that precious name,
Who built a throne of power
  Upon a cross of shame.

Unveil to me the beauty
  That glorifies his face—
The fullness of the father—
  The image of his grace.

My soul would run to meet Him;
  Restrain me not with creeds;
For Christ, the hope of glory,
  Is what my spirit needs.

I need the grand attraction,
  That centres 'round the cross,
To change the gilded things of earth,
  To emptiness and dross.

My feet are prone to wander,
  My eyes to turn aside,
And yet I fain would linger,
  With Christ the crucified.

I want a faith that's able
  To stand each storm and shock—
A faith forever rooted,
  In Christ the living Rock.

FIFTEENTH AMENDMENT

Beneath the burden of our joy
   Tremble, O wires, from East to West!
Fashion with words your tongues of fire,
   To tell the nation's high behest.

Outstrip the winds, and leave behind
   The murmur of the restless waves;
Nor tarry with your glorious news,
   Amid the ocean's coral caves.

Ring out! ring out! your sweetest chimes,
   Ye bells, that call to praise;
Let every heart with gladness thrill,
   And songs of joyful triumph raise.

Shake off the dust, O rising race!
   Crowned as a brother and a man;
Justice to-day asserts her claim,
   And from thy brow fades out the ban.

With freedom's chrism upon thy head,
   Her precious ensign in thy hand,
Go place thy once despised name
   Amid the noblest of the land.

A ransomed race! give God the praise,
   Who let thee through a crimson sea,
And 'mid the storm of fire and blood,
   Turned out the war-cloud's light to thee.

RETRIBUTION

Judgment slumbered. God in mercy
   Stayed his strong avenging hand;
Sent them priests and sent them prophets,
   But they would not understand.

Judgment lingered; men, grown bolder,
   Gloried in their shame and guilt;
And the blood of God's poor children
   Was as water freely spilt.

Then arose a cry to heaven,
   Deep and startling, sad and wild,
Sadder than the wail of Egypt,
   Mourning for the first-born child.

For the sighing of the needy
   God at length did bare his hand,
And the footsteps of his judgments
   Echoed through the guilty land.

Oh! the terror, grief and anguish;
   Oh! the bitter, fearful strife,
When the judgments of Jehovah
   Pressed upon the nation's life.

And the land did reel and tremble
   'Neath the terror of his frown,
For its guilt lay heavy on it,
   Pressing like an iron crown.

As a warning to the nations,
   Bathed in blood and swathed in fire,
Lay the once oppressing nation,
   Smitten by God's fearful ire.

THE SIN OF ACHAN

Night closed o'er the battl'ing army,
   But it brought them no success;
Victory perched not on their banners;
   Night was full of weariness.

Flushed and hopeful in the morning,
    Turned they from their leader's side:
Routed, smitten and defeated,
    Came they back at eventide.

Then in words of bitter mourning
    Joshua's voice soon arose:
"Tell us, O thou God of Jacob,
    Why this triumph of our foes?"

To his pleading came the answer
    Why the hosts in fear did yield:
"'Twas because a fearful trespass
    'Mid their tents did lie concealed."

Clear and plain before His vision,
    With whom darkness is as light,
Lay the spoils that guilty Achan
    Covered from his brethren's sight.

From their tents they purged the evil
    That had ruin round them spread;
Then they won the field of battle,
    Whence they had in terror fled.

Through the track of many ages
    Comes this tale of woe and crime;
Let us read it as a lesson
    And a warning for our time.

Oh, for some strong-hearted Joshua!
    Faithful to his day and time,
Who will wholly rid the nation
    Of her clinging curse and crime.

Till she writes on every banner
    All beneath these folds are free,
And the oppressed and groaning millions
    Shout the nation's Jubilee.

LINES TO MILES O'REILEY

You've heard no doubt of Irish bulls,
 And how they blunder, thick and fast;
But of all the queer and foolish things,
 O'Reiley, you have said the last.

You say we brought the rebs supplies,
 And gave them aid amid the fight,
And if you must be ruled by rebs,
 Instead of black you want them white.

You blame us that we did not rise,
 And pluck war from a fiery brand,
When Little Mac said if we did,
 He'd put us down with iron hand.

And when we sought to join your ranks,
 And battle with you, side by side,
Did men not curl their lips with scorn,
 And thrust us back with hateful pride?

And when at last we gained the field,
 Did we not firmly, bravely stand,
And help to turn the tide of death,
 That spread its ruin o'er the land?

We hardly think we're worse than those
 Who kindled up this fearful strife,
Because we did not seize the chance
 To murder helpless babes and wife.

And had we struck, with vengeful hand,
 The rebel where he most could feel,
Were you not ready to impale
 Out hearts upon your Northern steel?

O'Reiley, men like you should wear
    The gift of song, like some bright crown,
Nor worse than ruffians of the ring,
    Strike at a man because he's down.

THE LITTLE BUILDERS

Ye are builders little builders,
    Not with mortar, brick and stone,
But your work is far more glorious—
    Ye are building freedom's throne.

Where the ocean never slumbers
    Works the coral 'neath the spray,
By and by a reef or island
    Rears its head to greet the day.

When the balmy rains and sunshine
    Scatter treasures o'er the soil,
'Till a place for human footprints,
    Crown the little builder's toil.

When the stately ships sweep o'er them,
    Cresting all the sea with foam,
Little think these patient toilers,
    They are building man a home.

Do you ask me, precious children,
    How your little hands can build,
That you love the name of freedom,
    But your fingers are unskilled?

Not on thrones or in proud temples,
    Does fair freedom seek her rest;
No, her chosen habitations,
    Are the hearts that love her best.

Would you gain the highest freedom?
    Live for God and man alone,
Then each heart in freedom's temple
    Will be like a living stone.

Fill your minds with useful knowledge,
    Learn to love the true and right;
Thus you'll build the throne of freedom,
    On a pedestal of light.

THE DYING CHILD TO
HER BLIND FATHER

Dear father, I hear a whisper,
    It tells me that I must go,
And my heart returns her answer
    In throbbings so faint and low.

I'm sorry to leave you, father,
    I know you will miss me so,
And the world for you will gather
    A gloomier shade of woe.

You will miss me, dearest father,
    When the violets wake from sleep,
And timidly from their hedges
    The early snow-drops peep.

I shall not be here to gather
    The flowers by stream and dell,
The bright and beautiful flowers,
    Dear Father, you love so well.

You will miss my voice, dear father,
    From every earthly tone,
All the songs that cheered your darkness,
    And you'll be so sad and lone.

I can scarcely rejoice, dear father,
  In hope of the brighter land,
When I know you'll pine in sadness,
  And miss my guiding hand.

You are weeping, dearest father,
  Your sobs are shaking my soul,
But we'll meet again where the shadow
  And night from your eyes shall roll.

And then you will see me, father,
  With visions undimmed and clear,
Your eyes will sparkle with rapture—
  You know there's no blindness there.

LIGHT IN DARKNESS

We've room to build holy altars
  Where our crumbling idols lay;
We've room for heavenly visions,
  When our earth dreams fade away.

Through rifts and rents in our fortune
  We gaze with blinding tears,
Till glimpses of light and beauty
  Gilded our gloomy fears.

An angel stood at our threshold,
  We thought him a child of night,
Till we saw the print of his steps
  Made lines of living light.

We had much the world calls precious;
  We had heaps of shining dust;
We laid his hand on our treasures,
  And wrote on them moth and rust.

But still we had other treasures,
    That gold was too poor to buy,
We clasped them closer and closer,
    But saw them fade and die.

Our spirit grew faint and heavy,
    Deep shadows lay on our years,
Till light from the holy city,
    Streamed through our mist of tears.

And we thanked the chastening angel
    Who shaded our earthly light
For the light and beautiful visions
    That broke on our clearer sight.

Our first view of the Holy City
    Came through our darken'd years,
The songs that lightened our sorrows,
    We heard 'mid our night of tears.

OUR ENGLISH FRIENDS

Your land is crowned with regal men,
Whose brows ne'er wore a diadem,—
The men who, in our hour of need,
Reached out their hands and bade God speed.

Who watched across the distant strand
The anguish of our fainting land,
And grandly made our cause their own,
Till Slavery tottered on her throne.

When Slavery, full of wrath and strife,
Was clutching at the Nation's life,
How precious were your words of cheer
That fell upon the listening ear.

And when did fame, with glowing pen,
Record the deeds of nobler men,—
The men who, facing want and pain,
Loved freedom more than paltry gain.

O noble men! ye bravely stood
True to our country's highest good;
May God, who saw your aims and ends,
Forever bless our English friends!

AUNT CHLOE

I remember, well remember,
  That dark and dreadful day,
When they whispered to me, "Chloe,
  Your children's sold away!"

It seemed as if a bullet
  Had shot me through and through,
And I felt as if my heart-strings
  Was breaking right in two.

And I says to cousin Milly,
  "There must be some mistake;
Where's Mistus?" "In the great house crying—
  Crying like her heart would break.

"And the lawyer's there with Mistus;
  Says he's come to 'ministrate,
'Cause when master died he just left
  Heap of debt on the estate.

"And I thought 'twould do you good
  To bid your boys good-bye—
To kiss them both and shake their hands,
  And have a hearty cry.

"Oh! Chloe, I knows how you feel,
  'Cause I'se been through it all;
I thought my poor old heart would break,
  When master sold my Saul."

Just then I heard the footsteps
  Of my children at the door,
And then I rose right up to meet them,
  But I fell upon the floor.

And I heard poor Jakey saying,
  "Oh, mammy, don't you cry!"
And I felt my children kiss me
  And bid me, both, good-bye.

Then I had a mighty sorrow,
    Though I nursed it all alone;
But I wasted to a shadow,
    And turned to skin and bone.

But one day dear uncle Jacob
    (In heaven he's now a saint)
Said, "Your poor heart is in the fire,
    But child you must not faint."

Then I said to uncle Jacob,
    If I was good like you,
When the heavy trouble dashed me
    I'd know just what to do.

Then he said to me, "Poor Chloe,
    The way is open wide:"
And he told me of the Saviour,
    And the fountain in His side.

Then he said "Just take your burden
    To the blessed Master's feet;
I takes all my troubles, Chloe,
    Right unto the mercy-seat."

His words waked up my courage,
    And I began to pray,
And I felt my heavy burden
    Rolling like a stone away.

And a something seemed to tell me,
    You will see your boys again—
And that hope was like a poultice
    Spread upon a dreadful pain.

And it often seemed to whisper,
    Chloe, trust and never fear;
You'll get justice in the kingdom,
    If you do not get it here.

The Deliverance

Master only left old Mistus
   One bright and handsome boy;
But she fairly doted on him,
   He was her pride and joy.

We all liked Mister Thomas,
   He was so kind at heart;
And when the young folkes got in scrapes,
   He always took their part.

He kept right on that very way
   Till he got big and tall,
And old Mistus used to chide him
   And say he'd spile us all.

But somehow the farm did prosper
   When he took things in hand;
And though all the servants liked him,
   He made them understand.

One evening Mister Thomas said,
   "Just bring my easy shoes;
I am going to sit by mother,
   And read her up the news."

Soon I heard him tell old Mistus
   We're bound to have a fight;
But we'll whip the Yankees, mother,
   We'll whip them sure as night!"

Then I saw old Mistus tremble;
   She gasped and held her breath;
And she looked on Mister Thomas
   With a face as pale as death.

"They are firing on Fort Sumpter;
   Oh! I wish that I was there!—

Why, dear mother! what's the matter?
    You're the picture of despair."

"I was thinking, dearest Thomas,
    'Twould break my very heart
If a fierce and dreadful battle
    Should tear our lives apart."

"None but cowards, dearest mother,
    Would skulk unto the rear,
When the tyrant's hand is shaking
    All the heart is holding dear."

I felt sorry for old Mistus;
    She got too full to speak;
But I saw the great big tear-drops
    A running down her cheek.

Mister Thomas too was troubled
    With choosing on that night,
Betwixt staying with his mother
    And joining in the fight.

Soon down into the village came
    A call for volunteers;
Mistus gave up Mister Thomas,
    With many sighs and tears.

His uniform was real handsome;
    He looked so brave and strong;
But somehow I could'nt help thinking
    His fighting must be wrong.

Though the house was very lonesome,
    I thought 'twould all come right,
For I felt somehow or other
    We was mixed up in that fight.

And I said to Uncle Jacob,
 "How old Mistus feels the sting,
For this parting with your children
 Is a mighty dreadful thing."

"Never mind," said Uncle Jacob,
 "Just wait and watch and pray,
For I feel right sure and certain,
 Slavery's bound to pass away;

"Because I asked the Spirit,
 If God is good and just,
How it happened that the masters
 Did grind us to the dust.

"And something reasoned right inside,
 Such should not always be;
And you could not beat it out my head,
 The Spirit spoke to me."

And his dear old eyes would brighten,
 And his lips put on a smile,
Saying, "Pick up faith and courage,
 And just wait a little while."

Mistus prayed up in the parlor,
 That the Secesh all might win;
We were praying in the cabins,
 Wanting freedom to begin.

Mister Thomas wrote to Mistus,
 Telling 'bout the Bull's Run fight,
That his troops had whipped the Yankees
 And put them all to flight.

Mistus' eyes did fairly glisten;
 She laughed and praised the South,
But I thought some day she'd laugh
 On tother side her mouth.

I used to watch old Mistus' face,
   And when it looked quite long
I would say to Cousin Milly,
   The battle's going wrong;

Not for us, but for the Rebels.—
   My heart would fairly skip,
When Uncle Jacob used to say,
   "The North is bound to whip."

And let the fight go as it would—
   Let North or South prevail—
He always kept his courage up,
   And never let it fail.

And he often used to tell us,
   "Children, don't forget to pray;
For the darkest time of morning
   Is just 'fore the break of day."

Well, one morning bright and early
   We heard the fife and drum,
And the booming of the cannon—
   The Yankee troops had come.

When the word ran through the village,
   The colored folks are free—
In the kitchens and the cabins
   We held a jubilee.

When they told us Mister Lincoln
   Said that slavery was dead,
We just poured our prayers and blessings
   Upon his precious head.

We just laughed, and danced, and shouted
   And prayed, and sang, and cried,
And we thought dear Uncle Jacob
   Would fairly crack his side.

But when old Mistus heard it,
   She groaned and hardly spoke;
When she had to lose her servants,
   Her heart was almost broke.

'Twas a sight to see our people
   Going out, the troops to meet,
Almost dancing to the music,
   And marching down the street.

After years of pain and parting,
   Our chains was broke in two,
And we was so mighty happy,
   We did'nt know what to do.

But we soon got used to freedom,
   Though the way at first was rough;
But we weathered through the tempest,
   For slavery made us tough.

But we had one awful sorrow,
   It almost turned my head,
When a mean and wicked cretur
   Shot Mister Lincoln dead.

'Twas a dreadful solemn morning,
   I just staggered on my feet;
And the women they were crying
   And screaming in the street.

But if many prayers and blessings
   Could bear him to the throne,
I should think when Mister Lincoln died,
   That heaven just got its own.

Then we had another President,—
   What do you call his name?
Well, if the colored folks forget him
   They would'nt be much to blame.

We thought he'd be the Moses
    Of all the colored race;
But when the Rebels pressed us hard
    He never showed his face.

But something must have happened him,
    Right curi's I'll be bound,
'Cause I heard 'em talking 'bout a circle
    That he was swinging round.

But everything will pass away—
    He went like time and tide—
And when the next election came
    They let poor Andy slide.

But now we have a President,
    And if I was a man
I'd vote for him for breaking up
    The wicked Ku-Klux Klan.

And if any man should ask me
    If I would sell my vote,
I'd tell him I was not the one
    To change and turn my coat;

If freedom seem'd a little rough
    I'd weather through the gale;
And as to buying up my vote,
    I hadn't it for sale.

I do not think I'd ever be
    As slack as Jonas Handy;
Because I heard he sold his vote
    For just three sticks of candy.

But when John Thomas Reeder brought
    His wife some flour and meat,
And told he had sold his vote
    For something good to eat,

You ought to seen Aunt Kitty raise,
    And heard her blaze away;
She gave the meat and flour a toss,
    And said they should not stay.

And I should think he felt quite cheap
    For voting the wrong side;
And when Aunt Kitty scolded him,
    He just stood up and cried.

But the worst fooled man I ever saw,
    Was when poor David Rand
Sold out for flour and sugar;
    The sugar was mixed with sand.

I'll tell you how the thing got out;
    His wife had company,
And she thought the sand was sugar,
    And served it up for tea.

When David sipped and sipped the tea,
    Somehow it didn't taste right;
I guess when he found he was sipping sand
    He was mad enough to fight.

The sugar looked so nice and white—
    It was spread some inches deep—
But underneath was a lot of sand;
    Such sugar is mighty cheap.

You'd laughed to seen Lucinda Grange
    Upon her husband's track;
When he sold his vote for rations
    She made him take 'em back.

Day after day did Milly Green
    Just follow after Joe,
And told him if he voted wrong
    To take his rags and go.

I think that Samuel Johnson said
    His side had won the day,
Had not we women radicals
    Just got right in the way.

And yet I would not have you think
    That all our men are shabby;
But 'tis said in every flock of sheep
    There will be one that's scabby.

I've heard, before election came
    They tried to buy John Slade;
But he gave them all to understand
    That he wasn't in that trade.

And we've got lots of other men
    Who rally round the cause,
And go for holding up the hands
    That gave us equal laws,

Who know their freedom cost too much
    Of blood and pain and treasure,
For them to fool away their votes
    For profit or for pleasure.

Aunt Chloe's Politics

Of course, I don't know very much
    About these politics,
But I think that some who run 'em,
    Do mighty ugly tricks.

I've seen 'em honey-fugle round,
    And talk so awful sweet,
That you'd think them full of kindness
    As an egg is full of meat.

Now I don't believe in looking
  Honest people in the face,
And saying when you're doing wrong,
  That 'I haven't sold my race.'

When we want to school our children,
  If the money isn't there,
Whether black or white have took it,
  The loss we all must share.

And this buying up each other
  Is something worse than mean,
Though I thinks a heap of voting,
  I go for voting clean.

Learning to Read

Very soon the Yankee teachers
  Came down and set up school;
But, oh! how the Rebs did hate it,—
  It was agin' their rule.

Our masters always tried to hide
  Book learning from our eyes;
Knowledge did'nt agree with slavery—
  'Twould make us all too wise.

But some of us would try to steal
  A little from the book,
And put the words together,
  And learn by hook or crook.

I remember Uncle Caldwell,
  Who took pot liquor fat
And greased the pages of his book,
  And hid it in his hat.

And had his master ever seen
    The leaves upon his head,
He'd have thought them greasy papers,
    But nothing to be read.

And there was Mr. Turner's Ben,
    Who heard the children spell,
And picked the words right up by heart,
    And learned to read 'em well.

Well, the Northern folks kept sending
    The Yankee teachers down;
And they stood right up and helped us,
    Though Rebs did sneer and frown.

And I longed to read my Bible,
    For precious words it said;
But when I begun to learn it,
    Folks just shook their heads,

And said there is no use trying,
    Oh! Chloe, you're too late;
But as I was rising sixty,
    I had no time to wait.

So I got a pair of glasses,
    And straight to work I went,
And never stopped till I could read
    The hymns and Testament.

Then I got a little cabin
    A place to call my own—
And I felt as independent
    As the queen upon her throne.

Church Building

Uncle Jacob often told us,
    Since freedom blessed our race

We ought all to come together
  And build a meeting place.

So we pinched, and scraped, and spared,
  A little here and there:
Though our wages was but scanty,
  The church did get a share.

And, when the house was finished,
  Uncle Jacob came to pray;
He was looking mighty feeble,
  And his head was awful gray.

But his voice rang like a trumpet;
  His eyes looked bright and young;
And it seemed a mighty power
  Was resting on his tongue.

And he gave us all his blessing—
  'Twas parting words he said,
For soon we got the message
  The dear old man was dead.

But I believe he's in the kingdom,
  For when we shook his hand
He said, "Children, you must meet me
  Right in the promised land;

"For when I done a moiling
  And toiling here below,
Through the gate into the city
  Straightway I hope to go."

The Reunion

Well, one morning real early
  I was going down the street,
And I heard a stranger asking
  For Missis Chloe Fleet.

There was something in his voice
   That made me feel quite shaky.
And when I looked right in his face,
   Who should it be but Jakey!

I grasped him tight, and took him home—
   What gladness filled my cup!
And I laughed, and just rolled over,
   And laughed, and just give up.

"Where have you been? O Jakey, dear!
   Why didn't you come before?
Oh! when you children went away
   My heart was awful sore."

"Why, mammy, I've been on your hunt
   Since ever I've been free,
And I have heard from brother Ben,—
   He's down in Tennessee.

"He wrote me that he had a wife,"
   "And children?" "Yes, he's three."
"You married, too?" "Oh, no, indeed,
   I thought I'd first get free."

"Then, Jakey, you will stay with me,
   And comfort my poor heart;
Old Mistus got no power now
   To tear us both apart.

"I'm richer now than Mistus,
   Because I have got my son;
And Mister Thomas he is dead,
   And she's nary one.

"You must write to brother Benny
   That he must come this fall,
And we'll make the cabin bigger,
   And that will hold us all.

"Tell him I want to see 'em all
   Before my life do cease:
And then, like good old Simeon,
   I hope to die in peace."

I THIRST
First Voice

I thirst, but earth cannot allay
   The fever coursing through my veins,
The healing stream is far away—
   It flows through Salem's lovely plains.

The murmurs of its crystal flow
   Break ever o'er this world of strife;
My heart is weary, let me go,
   To bathe it in the stream of life;

For many worn and weary hearts
   Have bathed in this pure healing stream,
And felt their griefs and cares depart,
   E'en like some sad forgotten dream.

Second Voice

"The Word is nigh thee, even in thy heart."

Say not, within thy weary heart,
   Who shall ascend above,
To bring unto thy fever'd lips
   The fount of joy and love.

Nor do thou seek to vainly delve
   Where death's pale angels tread,
To hear the murmur of its flow
   Around the silent dead.

Within, in thee is the living fount,
    Fed from the springs above;
There quench thy thirst till thou shalt bathe
    In God's own sea of love.

THE DYING QUEEN

"I would meet death awake."

The strength that bore her on for years
    Was ebbing fast away,
And o'er the pale and life-worn face,
    Death's solemn shadows lay.

With tender love and gentle care,
    Friends gathered round her bed,
And for her sake each footfall hushed
    The echoes of its tread.

They knew the restlessness of death
    Through every nerve did creep,
And carefully they tried to lull
    The dying queen to sleep.

In vain she felt Death's icy hand
    Her failing heart-strings shake;
And, rousing up, she firmly said,
    "I'd meet my God awake."

Awake, I've met the battle's shock
    And born the cares of state;
Nor shall I take your lethean cup,
    And slumber at death's gate.

Did I not watch with eyes alert,
    The path where foes did tend;
And shall I veil my eyes with sleep,
    To meet my God and friend?

Nay, rather from my weary lids,
  This heavy slumber shake,
That I may pass the mystic vale
  And meet my God awake.

THE JEWISH GRANDFATHER'S STORY

Come, gather around me, children,
  And a story I will tell,
How we builded the beautiful temple—
  The temple we love so well.

I must date my story backward
  To a distant age and land,
When God did break our fathers' chains
  By his mighty outstretched hand.

Our fathers were strangers and captives,
  Where the ancient Nile doth flow;
Smitten by cruel taskmasters,
  And burdened by toil and woe.

As a shepherd, to pastures green
  Doth lead with care his sheep,
So God divided the great Red Sea,
  And led them through the deep.

You've seen me plant a tender vine,
  And guard it with patient care,
Till its roots struck in the mellow earth,
  And it drank the light and air.

So God did plant our chosen race.
  As vine in this fair land;
And we grew and spread a fruitful tree,
  The planting of his right hand.

The time would fail strove I to tell,
    All the story of our race—
Or our grand old leader, Moses,
    And Joshua in his place.

Of all our rulers and judges,
    From Joshua unto Saul,
Over whose doomed and guilty head
    Fell ruin and death's dark pall.

Of valiant Jepthath, whose brave heart
    With sudden grief did bow,
When his daughter came with dance and song
    Unconscious of his vow.

Of Gideon, lifting up his voice
    To him who rules the sky,
And wringing out his well drenched fleece
    When all around was dry.

How Deborah, neath her spreading palms,
    A judge in Israel rose,
And wrested victory from the hands
    Of Jacob's heathen foes.

Of Samuel, an upright judge,
    The last who ruled our tribes,
Whose noble life and cleanly hands,
    Were pure and free from bribes.

Of David, with his checkered life
    Our tuneful minstrel king,
Who breathed in sadness and delight,
    The psalms we love to sing.

Of Solomon, whose wandering heart,
    From Jacob's God did stray,
And cast the richest gifts of life,
    In pleasure's cup away.

How aged men advised his son,
    But found him weak and vain,
Until the kingdom from his hands
    Was rudely rent in twain.

Oh! sin and strife are fearful things,
    They widen as they go,
And leave behind them shades of death,
    And open gates of woe.

A trail of guilt, a gloomy line,
    Ran through our nation's life,
And wicked kings provoke our God,
    And sin and woe were rife.

At length, there came a day of doom—
    A day of grief and dread;
When judgment like a fearful storm
    Swept o'er our country's head.

And we were captives many years,
    Where Babel's stream doth flow;
With harps unstrung, on willows hung,
    We wept in silent woe.

We could not sing the old, sweet songs,
    Our captors asked to hear;
Our hearts were full, how could we sing
    The songs to us so dear?

As one who dreams a mournful dream,
    Which fades, as wanes the night,
So God did change our gloomy lot
    From darkness into light.

Belshazzar in his regal halls,
    A sumptuous feast did hold;
He praised his gods and drank his wine
    From sacred cups of gold.

When dance and song and revelry
　　Had filled with mirth each hall,
Belshazzar raised his eyes and saw
　　A writing on the wall.

He saw, and horror blanched his cheek,
　　His lips were white with fear;
To read the words he quickly called
　　For wise men, far and near.

But baffled seers, with anxious doubt
　　Stood silent in the room,
When Daniel came, a captive youth,
　　And read the words of doom.

That night, within his regal hall,
　　Belshazzar lifeless lay;
The Persians grasped his fallen crown
　　And with the Mede held sway.

Darius came, and Daniel rose
　　A man of high renown;
But wicked courtiers schemed and planned
　　To drag the prophet down.

They came as men who wished to place
　　Great honors on their king—
With flattering lips and oily words,
　　Desired a certain thing.

They knew that Daniel, day by day
　　Towards Salem turned his face,
And asked the king to sign a law
　　His hands might not erase.

That till one moon had waned away,
　　No cherished wish or thing
Should any ask of men or Gods,
　　Unless it were the king.

But Daniel, full of holy trust,
  His windows opened wide,
Regardless of the king's command,
  Unto his God he cried.

They brought him forth that he might be
  The hungry lion's meat,
Awe struck, the lions turned away
  And crouched near his feet.

The God he served was strong to save
  His servant in the den;
The fate devised for Daniel's life
  O'er took those scheming men.

And Cyrus came, a gracious King,
  And gave the blest command,
That we, the scattered Jews, should build
  Anew our Fallen land.

The men who hated Juda's weal
  Were filled with bitter rage,
And 'gainst the progress of our work
  Did evil men engage.

Sanballet tried to hinder us,
  And Gashmu uttered lies,
But like a thing of joy and light,
  We saw our temple rise.

And from the tower of Hananeel
  Unto the corner gate,
We built the wall and did restore
  The places desolate.

Some mocked us as we labored on
  And scoffingly did say,
"If but a fox climb on the wall,
  Their work will give away."

But Nehemiah wrought in hope,
　　Though heathen foes did frown
"My work is great," he firmly said,
　　"And I cannot come down."

And when Shemai counselled him
　　The temple door to close,
To hide, lest he should fall a prey
　　Unto his cruel foes.

Strong in his faith, he answered, No.
　　He would oppose the tide,
Should such as he from danger flee
　　And in the temple hide?

We wrought in earnest faith and hope
　　Until we build the wall,
And then, unto a joyful feast
　　Did priest and people call.

We came to dedicate the wall
　　With sacrifice and joy—
A happy throng, from aged sire
　　Unto the fair-haired boy.

Our lips so used to mournful songs,
　　Did joyous laughter fill,
And strong men wept with sacred joy
　　To stand on Zion's hill.

Mid scoffing foes and evil men,
　　We build our city blest,
And 'neath our sheltering vines and palms
　　To-day in peace we rest.

OUT IN THE COLD

Out in the cold mid the dreary night,
Under the eaves of homes so bright;
Snowflakes falling o'er mother's grave
Will no one rescue, no one save?

A child left out in the dark and cold,
A lamb not sheltered in any fold,
Hearing the wolves of hunger bark,
Out in the cold! and out in the dark.

Missing to-night the charming bliss
That lies in the mother's good-night kiss;
And hearing no loving father's prayer,
For blessings his children all may share.

Creeping away to some wretched den,
To sleep mid the curses of drunken men
And women, not as God has made,
Wretched and ruined, wronged and betrayed.

Church of the Lord reach thy arm,
And shield the hapless one from harm;
Where the waves of sin are dashing wild:
Rescue and save the drifting child.

Wash from her life guilt's turbid foam,
In the fair haven of a home;
Tenderly lead the motherless girl
Up to the gates of purest pearl.

The wandering feet which else had strayed,
From thorny paths may yet be stayed;
And a crimson track through the cold dark night
May exchange to a line of loving light.

SAVE THE BOYS

Like Dives in the deeps of Hell
I cannot break this fearful spell,
Nor quench the fires I've madly nursed,
Nor cool this dreadful raging thirst.
Take back your pledge—ye come too late!
Ye cannot save me from my fate,
Nor bring me back departed joys;
But ye can try to save the boys.

Ye bid me break my fiery chain,
Arise and be a man again,
When every street with snares is spread,
And nets of sin where'er I tread.
No; I must reap as I did sow.
The seeds of sin bring crops of woe;
But with my latest breath I'll crave
That ye will try the boys to save.

These bloodshot eyes were once so bright;
This sin-crushed heart was glad and light;
But by the wine-cup's ruddy glow
I traced a path to shame and woe.
A captive to my galling chain,
I've tried to rise, but tried in vain—
The cup allures and then destroys.
Oh! from its thraldom save the boys.

Take from your streets those traps of hell
Into whose gilded snares I fell.
Oh! freemen, from these foul decoys
Arise, and vote to save the boys.
Oh! ye who license men to trade
In draughts that charm and then degrade,
Before ye hear the cry, "Too late,"
Oh, save the boys from my sad fate.

NOTHING AND SOMETHING

"It is nothing to me," the beauty said,
With a careless toss of her pretty head;
"The man is weak if he can't refrain
From the cup you say is fraught with pain."
It was something to her in after years,
When her eyes were drenched with burning tears,
And she watched in lonely grief and dread,
And startled to hear a staggering tread.

"It is nothing to me," the mother said;
"I have no fear that my boy will tread
In the downward path of sin and shame,
And crush my heart and darken his name."
It was something to her when that only son
From the path of right was early won,
And madly cast in the flowing bowl
A ruined body and sin-wrecked soul.

"It is nothing to me," the young man cried:
In his eye was a flash of scorn and pride;
"I heed not the dreadful things ye tell:
I can rule myself I know full well."
It was something to him when in prison he lay
The victim of drink, life ebbing away;
And thought of his wretched child and wife,
And the mournful wreck of his wasted life.

"It is nothing to me," the merchant said,
As over his ledger he bent his head;
"I'm busy to-day with tare and tret,
And I have no time to fume and fret."
It was something to him when over the wire
A message came from a funeral pyre—
A drunken conductor had wrecked a train,
And his wife and child were among the slain.

"It is nothing to me," the voter said,
"The party's loss is my greatest dread";
Then gave his vote for the liquor trade,
Though hearts were crushed and drunkards made.
It was something to him in after life,
When his daughter became a drunkard's wife
And her hungry children cried for bread,
And trembled to hear their father's tread.

Is it nothing for us to idly sleep
While the cohorts of death their vigils keep?
To gather the young and thoughtless in,
And grind in our midst a grist of sin?
It is something, yes, all, for us to stand
Clasping by faith our Saviour's hand;
To learn to labor, live and fight
On the side of God and changeless light.

WANDERER'S RETURN

My home is so glad, my heart is so light,
My wandering boy has returned to-night.
He is blighted and bruised, I know, by sin,
But I am so glad to welcome him in.

The child of my tenderest love and care
Has broken away from the tempter's snare;
To-night my heart is o'erflowing with joy,
I have found again my wandering boy.

My heart has been wrung with a thousand fears,
Mine eyes been drenched with the bitterest tears;
Like shadows that fade are my past alarms,
My boy is enclasped in his mother's arms.

The streets were not safe for my darling child;
Where sin with its evil attractions smiled.
But his wandering feet have ceased to roam,
And to-night my wayward boy is at home—

At home with the mother that loves him best,
With the hearts that have ached with sad unrest,
With the hearts that are thrilling with untold joy
Because we have found our wandering boy.

In that wretched man so haggard and wild
I only behold my returning child,
And the blissful tears from my eyes that start
Are the overflow of a happy heart.

I have trodden the streets in lonely grief,
I have sought in prayer for my sole relief;
But the depths of my heart to-night are stirred,
I know that the mother's prayer has been heard.

If the mother-love be so strong and great
For her child, sin-weary and desolate,
Oh what must the love of the father be
For souls who have wandered like you and me!

FISHERS OF MEN

I had a dream, a varied dream:
   Before my ravished sight
The city of my Lord arose,
   With all its love and light.

The music of a myriad harps
   Flowed out with sweet accord;
And saints were casting down their crowns
   In homage to our Lord.

My heart leaped up with untold joy;
   Life's toil and pain were o'er;
My weary feet at last had found
   The bright and restful shore.

Just as I reached the gates of light,
   Ready to enter in,
From earth arose a fearful cry
   Of sorrow and of sin.

I turned, and saw behind me surge
   A wild and stormy sea;
And drowning men were reaching out
   Imploring hands to me.

And ev'ry lip was blanched with dread
   And moaning for relief;
The music of the golden harps
   Grew fainter for their grief.

Let me return, I quickly said.
   Close to the pearly gate;
My work is with these wretched ones,
   So wrecked and desolate.

An angel smiled and gently said:
   This is the gate of life,
Wilt thou return to earth's sad scenes,
   Its weariness and strife.

To comfort hearts that sigh and break,
   To dry the falling tear,
Wilt thou forego the music sweet
   Entrancing now thy ear?

I must return, I firmly said,
   The strugglers in that sea
Shall not reach out beseeching hands
   In vain for help to me.

I turned to go; but as I turned
  The gloomy sea grew bright,
And from my heart there seemed to flow
  Ten thousand cords of light.

And sin-wrecked men, with eager hands
  Did grasp each golden cord;
And with my heart I drew them on
  To see my gracious Lord.

Again I stood beside the gate.
  My heart was glad and free;
For with me stood a rescued throng
  The Lord had given me.

SIGNING THE PLEDGE

Do you see this cup—this tempting cup—
  Its sparkle and its glow?
I tell you this cup has brought to me
  A world of shame and woe.

Do you see that woman sad and wan?
  One day with joy and pride,
With orange blossoms in her hair,
  I claimed her as my bride.

And vowed that I would faithful prove
  Till death our lives should part;
I've drenched her soul with floods of grief,
  And almost crushed her heart.

Do you see that gray-haired mother bend
  Beneath her weight of years?
I've filled that aged mother's eyes
  With many bitter tears.

Year after year for me she prays,
  And tries her child to save;
I've almost brought her gray hairs down
  In sorrow to the grave.

Do you see that boy whose wistful eyes
  Are gazing on my face?
I've overshadowed his young life
  With sorrow and disgrace.

He used to greet me with a smile,
  His heart was light and glad;
I've seen him tremble at my voice,
  I've made that heart so sad.

Do you see this pledge I've signed to-night?
  My mother, wife, and boy
Shall read my purpose on that pledge
  And smile through tears of joy.

To know this night, this very night,
  I cast the wine-cup down,
And from the dust of a sinful life
  Lift up my manhood's crown.

The faded face of my young wife
  With roses yet shall bloom,
And joy shall light my mother's eyes
  On the margin of the tomb.

I have vowed to-night my only boy,
  With brow so fair and mild,
Shall not be taunted on the streets,
  And called a drunkard's child.

Never again shall that young face
  Whiten with grief and dread,
Because I've madly staggered home
  And sold for drink his bread.

This strong right arm unnerved by rum
  Shall battle with my fate;
And peace and comfort crown the home
  By drink made desolate.

Like a drowning man, tempest-tossed,
  Clings to a rocky ledge,
With trembling hands I've learned to grasp
  The gospel and the pledge.

A captive bounding from my chain,
  I've rent each hateful band,
And by the help of grace divine
  A victor hope to stand.

THE MARTYR OF ALABAMA

(The following news item appeared in the newspapers throughout the country, issue of December 27, 1894:

"Tim Thompson, a little negro boy, was asked to dance for the amusement of some white toughs. He refused, saying he was a church member. One of the men knocked him down with a club and then danced upon his prostrate form. He then shot the boy in the hip. The boy is dead; his murderer is still at large.")

He lifted up his pleading eyes,
  And scanned each cruel face,
Where cold and brutal cowardice
  Had left its evil trace.

It was when tender memories
  Round Beth'lem's manger lay,
And mothers told their little ones
  Of Jesu's natal day.

And of the Magi from the East
   Who came their gifts to bring,
And bow in rev'rence at the feet
   Of Salem's new-born King.

And how the herald angels sang
   The choral song of peace,
That war should close his wrathful lips,
   And strife and carnage cease.

At such an hour men well may hush
   Their discord and their strife,
And o'er that manger clasp their hands
   With gifts to brighten life.

Alas! that in our favored land,
   That cruelty and crime
Should cast their shadows o'er a day,
   The fairest pearl of time.

A dark-browed boy had drawn anear
   A band of savage men,
Just as a hapless lamb might stray
   Into a tiger's den.

Cruel and dull, they saw in him
   For sport an evil chance,
And then demanded of the child
   To give to them a dance.

"Come dance for us" the rough men said;
   "I can't," the child replied,
"I cannot for the dear Lord's sake,
   Who for my sins once died."

Tho they were strong and he was weak,
   He wouldn't his Lord deny,
His life lay in their cruel hands,
   But he for Christ could die.

Heard they aright? Did that brave child
   Their mandates dare resist?
Did he against their stern commands
   Have courage to resist?

Then recklessly a man(?) arose,
   And dealt a fearful blow.
He crushed the portals of that life,
   And laid the brave child low.

And trampled on his prostrate form,
   As on a broken toy;
Then danced with careless, brutal feet,
   Upon the murdered boy.

Christians! behold that martyred child!
   His blood cries from the ground;
Before the sleepless eye of God,
   He shows each gaping wound.

Oh! Church of Christ arise! arise!
   Let crimson stain thy hand,
When God shall inquisition make
   For blood shed in the land.

Take sackcloth of the darkest hue,
   And shroud the pulpit round;
Servants of him who cannot lie
   Sit mourning on the ground.

Let holy horror blanch each brow,
   Pale every cheek with fears,
And rocks and stones, if ye could speak,
   Ye well might melt to tears.

Through every fane send forth a cry,
   Of sorrow and regret,
Nor in an hour of careless ease
   Thy brother's wrongs forget.

Veil not thine eyes, nor close thy lips,
   Nor speak with bated breath;
This evil shall not always last,—
   The end of it is death.

Avert the doom that crime must bring
   Upon a guilty land;
Strong in the strength that God supplies,
   For truth and justice stand.

For Christless men, with reckless hands,
   Are sowing around thy path
The tempests wild that yet shall break
   In whirlwinds of God's wrath.

THE NIGHT OF DEATH

'Twas a night of dreadful horror,—
   Death was sweeping through the land;
And the wings of dark destruction
   Were outstretched from strand to strand.

Strong men's hearts grew faint with terror,
   As the tempest and the waves
Wrecked their homes and swept them downward,
   Suddenly to yawning graves.

'Mid the wastes of ruined households,
   And the tempest's wild alarms,
Stood a terror-stricken mother
   With a child within her arms.

Other children huddled 'round her,
   Each one nestling in her heart;
Swift in thought and swift in action,
   She at least from one must part.

Then she said unto her daughter,
    "Strive to save one child from death."
"Which one?" said the anxious daughter,
    As she stood with bated breath.

Oh! the anguish of that mother;
    What despair was in her eye!
All her little ones were precious;
    Which one should she leave to die?

Then outspake the brother Bennie:
    "I will take the little one."
"No," exclaimed the anxious mother;
    "No, my child, it can't be done."

"See! my boy, the waves are rising,
    Save yourself and leave the child!"
"I will trust in Christ," he answered;
    Grasped the little one and smiled.

Through the roar of wind and waters
    Ever and anon she cried;
But throughout the night of terror
    Never Bennie's voice replied.

But above the waves' wild surging
    He had found a safe retreat,
As if God had sent an angel,
    Just to guide his wandering feet.

When the storm had spent its fury,
    And the sea gave up its dead,
She was mourning for her loved ones,
    Lost amid that night of dread.

While her head was bowed in anguish,
    On her ear there fell a voice,
Bringing surcease to her sorrow,
    Bidding all her heart rejoice.

"Didn't I tell you true?" said Bennie,
    And his eyes were full of light,
"When I told you God would help me
    Through the dark and dreadful night?"

And he placed the little darling
    Safe within his mother's arms,
Feeling Christ had been his guardian,
    'Mid the dangers and alarms.

Oh! for faith so firm and precious,
    In the darkest, saddest night,
Till life's gloom-encircled shadows
    Fade in everlasting light.

And upon the mount of vision
    We our loved and lost shall greet,
With earth's wildest storms behind us,
    And its cares beneath our feet.

MOTHER'S TREASURES

Two little children sit by my side,
    I call them Lily and Daffodil;
I gaze on them with a mother's pride,
    One is Edna, the other is Will.

Both have eyes of starry light,
    And laughing lips o'er teeth of pearl.
I would not change for a diadem
    My noble boy and darling girl.

To-night my heart o'erflows with joy;
    I hold them as a sacred trust;
I fain would hide them in my heart,
    Safe from tarnish of moth and rust.

What should I ask for my dear boy?
    The richest gifts of wealth or fame?
What for my girl? A loving heart
    And a fair and spotless name?

What for my boy? That he should stand
    A pillar of strength to the state?
What for my girl? That she should be
    The friend of the poor and desolate?

I do not ask they shall never tread
    With weary feet the paths of pain.
I ask that in the darkest hour
    They may faithful and true remain.

I only ask their lives may be
    Pure as gems in the gates of pearl,
Lives to brighten and bless the world—
    This I ask for my boy and girl.

I ask to clasp their hands again
    'Mid the holy hosts of heaven,
Enraptured say: "I am here, oh! God,
    And the children Thou has given."

THE REFINER'S GOLD

He stood before my heart's closed door,
    And asked to enter in;
But I had barred the passage o'er
    By unbelief and sin.

He came with nail-prints in his hands,
    To set my spirit free;
With wounded feet he trod a path
    To come and sup with me.

He found me poor and brought me gold,
    The fire of love had tried,
And garments whitened by his blood,
    My wretchedness to hide.

The glare of life had dimmed my eyes,
    Its glamour was too bright.
He came with ointment in his hands
    To heal my darkened sight.

He knew my heart was tempest-tossed,
    By care and pain oppressed;
He whispered to my burdened heart,
    Come unto me and rest.

He found me weary, faint and worn,
    On barren mountains cold;
With love's constraint he drew me on,
    To shelter in his fold.

Oh! foolish heart, how slow wert thou
    To welcome thy dear guest,
To change thy weariness and care
    For comfort, peace and rest.

Close to his side, oh! may I stay,
    Just to behold his face,
Till I shall wear within my soul
    The image of his grace.

The grace that changes hearts of stone
    To tenderness and love,
And bids us run with willing feet
    Unto his courts above.

A STORY OF THE REBELLION

The treacherous sands had caught our boat,
    And held it with a strong embrace
And death at our imprisoned crew
    Was sternly looking face to face.

With anxious hearts, but failing strength,
    We strove to push the boat from shore;
But all in vain, for there we lay
    With bated breath and useless oar.

Around us in a fearful storm
    The fiery hail fell thick and fast;
And we engirded by the sand,
    Could not return the dreadful blast.

When one arose upon whose brow
    The ardent sun had left his trace;
A noble purpose strong and high
    Uplighting all his dusky face.

Perchance within that fateful hour
    The wrongs of ages thronged apace;
But with it came the glorious hope
    Of swift deliverance to his race.

Of galling chains asunder rent,
    Of severed hearts again made one,
Of freedom crowning all the land
    Through battles gained and victories won.

"Some one," our hero firmly said,
    "Must die to get us out of this;"
Then leaped upon the strand and bared
    His bosom to the bullets' hiss.

"But ye are soldiers, and can fight,
    May win in battles yet unfought;
I have no offering but my life,
    And if they kill me it is nought."

With steady hands he grasped the boat,
    And boldly pushed it from the shore;
Then fell by rebel bullets pierced,
    His life work grandly, nobly o'er.

Our boat was rescued from the sands
    And launched in safety on the tide;
But he our comrade good and grand,
    In our defence had bravely died.

BURIAL OF SARAH

He stood before the sons of Heth,
    And bowed his sorrowing head;
"I've come," he said, "to buy a place
    Where I may lay my dead.

"I am a stranger in your land,
    My home has lost its light;
Grant me a place where I may lay
    My dead away from sight."

Then tenderly the sons of Heth
    Gazed on the mourner's face,
And said, "Oh, Prince, amid our dead,
    Choose thou her resting-place.

"The sepulchres of those we love,
    We place at thy command;
Against the plea thy grief hath made
    We close not heart nor hand."

The patriarch rose and bowed his head,
    And said, "One place I crave;
'Tis at the end of Ephron's field,
    And called Machpelah's cave.

"Entreat him that he sell to me
    For her last sleep that cave;
I do not ask for her I loved
    The freedom of a grave."

The son of Zohar answered him,
    "Hearken, my lord, to me;
Before our sons, the field and cave
    I freely give to thee."

"I will not take it as a gift,"
    The grand old man then said;
"I pray thee let me buy the place
    Where I may lay my dead."

And with the promise in his heart,
    His seed should own that land,
He gave the shekels for the field
    He took from Ephron's hand.

And saw afar the glorious day
    His chosen seed should tread,
The soil where he in sorrow lay
    His loved and cherished dead.

GOING EAST

She came from the East a fair, young bride,
    With a light and bounding heart,
To find in the distant West a home
    With her husband to make a start.

He builded his cabin far away,
    Where the prairie flower bloomed wild;
Her love made lighter all his toil,
    And joy and hope around him smiled.

She plied her hands to life's homely tasks,
    And helped to build his fortunes up;
While joy and grief, like bitter and sweet,
    Were mingled and mixed in her cup.

He sowed in his fields of golden grain,
    All the strength of his manly prime;
Nor music of bides, nor brooks, nor bees,
    Was as sweet as the dollar's chime.

She toiled and waited through weary years
    For the fortune that came at length;
But toil and care and hope deferred,
    Had stolen and wasted her strength.

The cabin changed to a stately home,
    Rich carpets were hushing her tread;
But light was fading from her eye,
    And the bloom from her cheek had fled.

Her husband was adding field to field,
    And new wealth to his golden store;
And little thought the shadow of death
    Was entering in at his door.

Slower and heavier grew her step,
    While his gold and his gains increased;
But his proud domain had not the charm
    Of her humble home in the East.

He had no line to sound the depths
    Of her tears repressed and unshed;
Nor dreamed 'mid plenty a human heart
    Could be starving, but not for bread.

Within her eye was a restless light,
  And a yearning that never ceased,
A longing to see the dear old home
  She had a left in the distant East.

A longing to clasp her mother's hand,
  And nestle close to her heart,
And to feel the heavy cares of life
  Like the sun-kissed shadows depart.

The hungry heart was stilled at last;
  Its restless, baffled yearning ceased.
A lonely man sat by the bier
  Of a corpse that was going East.

THE HERMIT'S SACRIFICE

From Rome's palaces and villas
  Gaily issued forth a throng;
From her humbler habitations
  Moved a human tide along.

Haughty dames and blooming maidens,
  Men who knew not mercy's sway,
Thronged into the Coliseum
  On that Roman holiday.

From the lonely wilds of Asia,
  From her jungles far away,
From the distant torrid regions,
  Rome had gathered beasts of prey.

Lions restless, roaring, rampant,
  Tigers with their stealthy tread,
Leopards bright, and fierce, and fiery,
  Met in conflict wild and dread.

Fierce and fearful was the carnage
  Of the maddened beasts of prey,
As they fought and rent each other
  Urged by men more fierce than they.

Till like muffled thunders breaking
  On a vast and distant shore,
Fainter grew the yells of tigers,
  And the lions' dreadful roar.

On the crimson-stained arena
  Lay the victims of the fight;
Eyes which once had glared with anguish,
  Lost in death their baleful light.

Then uprose the gladiators
  Armed for conflict unto death,
Waiting for the prefect's signal,
  Cold and stern with bated breath.

"Ave Caesar, morituri,
  Te, sulatant," rose the cry
From the lips of men ill-fated,
  Doomed to suffer and to die.

Then began the dreadful contest,
  Lives like chaff were thrown away,
Rome with all her pride and power
  Butchered for a holiday.

Eagerly the crowd were waiting,
  Loud the clashing sabres rang,
When between the gladiators
  All unarmed a hermit sprang.

"Cease your bloodshed," cried the hermit,
  "On this carnage place your ban;"
But with flashing swords they answered,
  "Back unto your place, old man."

From their path the gladiators
   Thrust the strange intruder back,
Who between their hosts advancing
   Calmly parried their attack.

All undaunted by their weapons,
   Stood the old heroic man;
While a maddened cry of anger
   Through the vast assembly ran.

"Down with him," cried out the people,
   As with thumbs unbent they glared,
Till the prefect gave the signal
   That his life should not be spared.

Men grew wild with wrathful passion,
   When his fearless words were said
Cruelly they fiercely showered
   Stones on his devoted head.

Bruised and bleeding fell the hermit,
   Victor in that hour of strife;
Gaining in his death a triumph
   That he could not win in life.

Had he uttered on the forum
   Struggling thoughts within him born,
Men had jeered his words as madness,
   But his deed they could not scorn.

Not in vain had been his courage,
   Nor for naught his daring deed;
From his grave his mangled body
   Did for wretched captives plead.

From that hour Rome, grown more thoughtful,
   Ceased her sport in human gore;
And into her Coliseum
   Gladiators came no more.

SONGS FOR THE PEOPLE

Let me make the songs for the people,
　　Songs for the old and young;
Songs to stir like a battle-cry
　　Wherever they are sung.

Not for the clashing of sabres,
　　Nor carnage nor for strife;
But songs to thrill the hearts of men
　　With more abundant life.

Let me make the songs for the weary,
　　Amid life's fever and fret,
Till hearts shall relax their tension,
　　And careworn brows forget.

Let me sing for little children,
　　Before their footsteps stray,
Sweet anthems of love and duty,
　　To float o'er life's highway.

I would sing for the poor and aged,
　　When shadows dim their sight;
Of the bright and restful mansions,
　　Where there shall be no night.

Our world, so worn and weary,
　　Needs music, pure and strong,
To hush the jangle and discords
　　Of sorrow, pain, and wrong.

Music to soothe all its sorrow,
　　Till war and crime shall cease;
And the hearts of men grown tender
　　Girdle the world with peace.

THEN AND NOW

"Build me a nation," said the Lord.
The distant nations heard the word,
"Build me a nation true and strong,
Bar out the old world's hate and wrong;"
For men had traced with blood and tears
The trail of weary wasting years,
And torn and bleeding martyrs trod
Through fire and torture up to God.

While in the hollow of his hand
God hid the secret of our land,
Men warred against their fiercest foes,
And kingdoms fell and empires rose,
Till, weary of the old world strife,
Men sought for broader, freer life,
And plunged into the ocean's foam
To find another, better home.

And, like a vision fair and bright,
The new world broke upon their sight.
Men grasped the prize, grew proud and strong,
And cursed the land with crime and wrong.
The Indian stood despoiled of lands,
The Negro bound with servile hands,
Oppressed through weary years of toil.
His blood and tears bedewed the soil.

Then God arose in dreadful wrath,
And judgment streamed around his path;
His hand the captive's fetters broke,
His lightnings shattered every yoke.
As Israel through the Red sea trod,
Led by the mighty hand of God,
They passed to freedom through a flood,
Whose every wave and surge was blood.

And slavery, with its crime and shame,
Went down in wrath and blood and flame.
The land was billowed o'er with graves
Where men had lived and died as slaves.
Four and thirty years—what change since then!
Beings once chattles now are men;
Over the gloom of slavery's night,
Has flashed the dawn of freedom's light.

To-day no mother with anguish wild
Kneels and implores that her darling child
Shall not be torn from her bleeding heart,
With its quivering tendrils rent apart.
The father may sooth his child to sleep,
And watch his slumbers calm and deep.
No tyrant's tread will disturb his rest
Where freedom dwells as a welcome guest.

His walls may be bare of pictured grace,
His fireside the lowliest place;
But the wife and children sheltered there
Are his to defend and guard with care.
Where haughty tyrants once bore rule
Are ballot-box and public school.
The old slave-pen of former days
Gives place to fanes of prayer and praise.

To-night we would bring our meed of praise
To noble friends of darker days;
The men and women crowned with light,
The true and tried in our gloomy night.
To Lundy, whose heart was early stirred
To speak for freedom an earnest word;
To Carrison, valiant, true and strong,
Whose face was as flight against our wrong.

And Phillips, the peerless, grand and brave,
A tower of strength to the outcast slave.

Earth has no marble too pure and white
To enroll his name in golden light.
Our Douglass, too, with his broken chain,
Who plead our cause with his broken chain,
And helped to hurl from his bloody seat
The curse that writhed and died at his feet.

And Governor Andrew, who, looking back,
Saw none he despised, though poor and black;
And Harriet Beecher, whose glowing pen
Corroded the chains of fettered men.
To-night with greenest laurels we'll crown
North Elba's grave where sleeps John Brown,
Who made the gallows an altar high,
And showed how a brave old man could die.
And Lincoln, our martyred President.
Who returned to his God with chains he had rent.
And Sumner, amid death's icy chill,
Leaving to Hoar his Civil Rights Bill.
And let us remember old underground,
With all her passengers northward bound,
The train that ran till it ceased to pay,
With all her dividends given away.

Nor let it be said that we have forgot
The women who stood with Lucretia Mott;
Nor her who to the world was known
By the simple name of Lucy Stone.
A tribute unto a host of others
Who knew that men though black were brothers,
Who battered against our nation's sin,
Whose graves are thick whose rank are thin.
Oh, people chastened in the fire,
To nobler, grander things aspire;
In the new era of your life,
Bring love for hate, and peace for strife;
Upon your hearts this vow record

That ye will build unto the Lord
A nobler future, true and grand,
To strengthen, crown and bless the land.
A higher freedom ye may gain
Than that which comes from a riven chain;
Freedom your native land to bless,
With peace, and love and righteousness,
As dreams that are past, a tale all told,
Are the days when men were bought and sold;
Now God be praised from sea to sea,
Our flag floats o'er a country free.

MACEO

Maceo dead! a thrill of sorrow
    Through our hearts in sadness ran
When we felt in one sad hour
    That the world had lost a man.

He had clasped unto his bosom
    The sad fortunes of his land—
Held the cause for which he perished
    With a firm, unfaltering hand.

On his lips the name of freedom
    Fainted with his latest breath.
"Cuba libre" was his watchword
    Passing through the gates of death.

With the light of God around us,
    Why this agony and strife?
With the cross of Christ before us,
    Why this fearful waste of life?

Must the pathway unto freedom
    Ever mark a crimson line,
And the eyes of wayward mortals
    Always close to light divine?

Must the heart of fearless valor
    Fail 'mid crime and cruel wrong,
When the world has read of heroes
    Brave and earnest, true and strong?

None to stay the floods of sorrow
    Sweeping round each war-crushed heart;
Men to say to strife and carnage—
    From our world henceforth depart.

God of peace and God of nations,
    Haste! oh, haste the glorious day
When the reign of our Redeemer
    O'er the world shall have its sway.

When the swords now blood encrusted,
    Spears that reap the battle field,
Shall be charged to higher service,
    Helping earth reach harvest yield.

Where the widow weeps in anguish,
    And the orphan bows his head,
Grant that peace and joy and gladness
    May like holy angels tread.

Pity, oh, our God the sorrow
    Of thy world from thee astray,
Lead us from the paths of madness
    Unto Christ the living way.

Year by year the world grows weary
    'Neath its weight of sin and strife,
Though the hands once pierced and bleeding
    Offer more abundant life.

May the choral song of angels
    Heard upon Judea's plain
Sound throughout the earth the tidings
    Of that old and sweet refrain.

Till our world, so sad and weary,
    Finds the balmy rest of peace—
Peace to silence all her discords—
    Peace till war and crime shall cease.

Peace to fall like gentle showers,
    As on parched flowers dew,
Till our hearts proclaim with gladness:
    Lo, He maketh all things new.

ONLY A WORD

Only a word, a friendly word,
    Tender and kind and true;
A fainting heart drank in the word,
    As flowers absorb the dew.

Only a word, a faithful word,
    Feet that had gone astray
Were pointed from the trend of death
    Unto the narrow way.

A tender, loving, earnest word,
    Sown mid prayers and tears
May bloom in time and fruitage
    Throughout eternal years.

MY MOTHER'S KISS

My mother's kiss, my mother's kiss,
    I feel its impress now;
As in the bright and happy days
    She pressed it on my brow.

You may see it is a fancied thing
  Within my memory fraught;
To me it has a sacred place—
  The treasure house of thought.

Again, I feel her fingers glide
  Amid my clustering hair;
I see the love-light in her eyes,
  When all my life was fair.

Again, I hear her gentle voice
  In warning or in love.
How precious was the faith that taught
  My soul of things above.

The music of her voice is stilled.
  Her lips are paled in death.
As precious pearls I'll clasp her words
  Until my latest breath.

The world had scattered round my path
  Honor and wealth and fame;
But naught so precious as the thoughts
  That gather round her name.

And friends have placed upon my brow
  The laurels of renown;
But she first taught me how to wear
  My manhood as a crown.

My hair is silvered o'er with age,
  I'm longing to depart;
To clasp again my mother's hand,
  And be a child at heart.

To roam with her the glory-land
  Where saints and angels greet;
To cast our crowns with songs of love
  At our Redeemer's feet.

A GRAIN OF SAND

Do you see this grain of sand
Lying loosely in my hand?
Do you know to me it brought
Just a simple loving thought?
When one gazes night by night
On the glorious stars of light,
Oh how little seems the span
Measured round the life of man.

Oh! how fleeting are his years
With their smiles and their tears;
Can it be that God does care
For such atoms as we are?
Then outspake this grain of sand
"I was fashioned by His hand.
In the star lit realms of space
I was made to have a place.

"Should the ocean flood the world,
Were its mountains 'gainst me hurled.
All the force they could employ
Wouldn't a single grain destroy;
And if I, a thing so light,
Have a place within His sight;
You are linked unto his throne
Cannot live nor die alone.

"In the everlasting arms
Mid life's dangers and alarms
Let calm trust your spirit fill;
Know He's God, and then be still."
Trustingly I raised my head
Hearing what the atom said;
Knowing man is greater far
Than the brightest sun or star.

THE CROCUSES

They heard the South wind sighing
  A murmur of the rain;
And they knew that Earth was longing
  To see them all again.

While the snow-drops still were sleeping
  Beneath the silent sod;
They felt their new life pulsing
  Within the dark, cold clod.

Not a daffodil nor daisy
  Had dared to raise its head;
Not a fairhaired dandelion
  Peeped timid from its bed;

Though a tremor of the winter
  Did shivering through them run;
Yet they lifted up their foreheads
  To greet the vernal sun.

And the sunbeams gave them welcome,
  As did the morning air
And scattered o'er their simple robes
  Rich tints of beauty rare.

Soon a host of lovely flowers
  From vales and woodland burst;
But in all that fair procession
  The crocuses were first.

First to weave for Earth a chaplet
  To crown her dear old head
And to beautify the pathway
  Where winter still did tread.

And their loved and white haired mother
    Smiled sweetly 'neath the tough,
When she knew her faithful children
    Were loving her so much.

THE PRESENT AGE

Say not the age is hard and cold—
    I think it brave and grand;
When men of diverse sects and creeds
    Are clasping hand in hand.

The Parsee from his sacred fires
    Beside the Christian kneels;
And clearer light to Islam's eyes
    The word of Christ reveals.

The Brahmin from his distant home
    Brings thoughts of ancient lore;
The Bhuddist breaking bonds of caste
    Divides mankind no more.

The meek-eyed sons of far Cathay
    Are welcome round the board;
Not greed, nor malice drives away
    These children of our Lord.

And Judah from whose trusted hands
    Came oracles divine;
Now sits with those around whose hearts
    The light of God doth shine.

Japan unbars her long sealed gates
    From islands far away;
Her sons are lifting up their eyes
    To greet the coming day.

The Indian child from forests wild
   Has learned to read and pray;
The tomahawk and scalping knife
   From him have passed away.

From centuries of servile toil
   The Negro finds release,
And builds the fanes of prayer and praise
   Unto the God of Peace.

England and Russia face to face
   With Central Asia meet;
And on the far Pacific coast
   Chinese and natives greet.

Crusaders once with sword and shield
   The Holy Land to save;
From Moslem hands did strive to clutch
   The dear Redeemer's grave.

A battle greater, grander far
   Is for the present age;
A crusade for the rights of man
   To brighten history's page.

Where labor faints and bows her head,
   And want consorts with crime;
Or men grown faithless sadly say
   That evil is the time.

There is the field, the vantage ground
   For every earnest heart;
To side with justice, truth and right
   And act a noble part.

To save from ignorance and vice
   The poorest, humblest child;
To make our age the fairest one
   On which the sun has smiled;

To plant the roots of coming years
　　In mercy, love and truth;
And bid our weary, saddened earth
　　Again renew her youth.

Oh! earnest hearts! toil on in hope,
　　'Till darkness shrinks from light;
To fill the earth with peace and joy,
　　Let youth and age unite;

To stay the floods of sin and shame
　　That sweep from shore to shore;
And furl the banners strained with blood,
　　'Till war shall be no more.

Blame not the age, nor think it full
　　Of evil and unrest;
But say of every other age,
　　"This one shall be the best."

The age to brighten every path
　　By sin and sorrow trod;
For loving hearts to usher in
　　The commonwealth of God.

DEDICATION POEM

　　Dedication Poem on the reception of the annex to the home for aged colored people, from the bequest of Mr. Edward T. Parker.

Outcast from her home in Syria
　　In the lonely, dreary wild;
Heavy hearted, sorrow stricken,
　　Sat a mother and her child.

There was not a voice to cheer her
    Not a soul to share her fate;
She was weary, he was fainting,
    And life seemed so desolate.

Far away in sunny Egypt
    Was lone Hagar's native land;
Where the Nile in kingly bounty
    Scatters bread throughout the land.

In the tents of princely Abram
    She for years had found a home;
Till the stern decree of Sarah
    Sent her forth the wild to roam.

Hour by hour she journeyed onward
    From the shelter of their tent
Till her footsteps slowly faltered
    And the water all was spent;

Then she veiled her face in sorrow,
    Feared her child would die of thirst;
Till her eyes with tears so holden
    Saw a sparkling fountain burst.

Oh! how happy was that mother,
    What a soothing of her pain;
When she saw her child reviving,
    Life rejoicing through each vein.

Does not life repeat this story,
    Tell it over day by day?
Of the fountain of refreshment
    Ever springing by our way.

Here is one by which we gather,
    On this bright and happy day.
Just to bask beside a fountain
    Making gladder life's highway.

Bringing unto hearts now aged
    Who have borne life's burdens long,
Such a gift of love and mercy
    As deserves our sweetest song.

Such a gift that even heaven
    May rejoice with us below,
If the pure and holy angels
    Join us in our joy and woe.

May the memory of the giver
    In this home where age may rest,
Float like fragrance through the ages,
    Ever blessing, ever blest.

When the gates of pearl are opened
    May we there this friend behold
Drink with him from living fountains,
    Walk with him the streets of gold.

When life's shattered cords of music
    Shall again be sweetly sung;
Then our hearts with life immortal,
    Shall be young, forever young.

A DOUBLE STANDARD

Do you blame me that I loved him?
    If when standing all alone
I cried for bread a careless world
    Pressed to my lips a stone.

Do you blame me that I loved him,
    That my heart beat glad and free,
When he told me in the sweetest tones
    He loved but only me?

Can you blame me that I did not see
   Beneath his burning kiss
The serpent's wiles, nor even hear
   The deadly adder hiss?

Can you blame me that my heart grew cold
   That the tempted, tempter turned;
When he was feted and caressed
   And I was coldly spurned?

Would you blame him, when you draw from me
   Your dainty robes aside.
If he with gilded baits should claim
   Your fairest as his bride?

Would you blame the world if it should press
   On him a civic crown;
And see me struggling in the depth
   Then harshly press me down?

Crime has no sex and yet to-day
   I wear the brand of shame;
Whilst he amid the gay and proud
   Still bears an honored name.

Can you blame me if I've learned to think
   Your hate of vice a sham,
When you so coldly crushed me down
   And then excused the man?

Would you blame me if to-morrow
   The coroner should say,
A wretched girl, outcast, forlorn,
   Has thrown her life away?

Yes, blame me for my downward course,
   But oh! remember well,
Within your homes you press the hand
   That led me down to hell.

I'm glad God's ways are not our ways,
　　He does not see as man,
Within His love I know there's room
　　For those whom others ban.

I think before His great white throne,
　　His throne of spotless light,
That whited sepulchres shall wear
　　The hue of endless night.

That I who fell, and he who sinned,
　　Shall reap as we have sown;
That each the burden of his loss
　　Must bear and bear alone.

No golden weights can turn the scale
　　Of justice in His sight;
And what is wrong in woman's life
　　In man's cannot be right.

OUR HERO

Onward to her destination,
　　O'er the stream the Hannah sped,
When a cry of consternation
　　Smote and chilled our hearts with dread.

Wildly leaping, madly sweeping,
　　all relentless in their sway,
Like a band of cruel demons
　　Flames were closing 'round our way.

Oh! the horror of those moments;
　　Flames above and waves below—
Oh! the agony of ages
　　Crowded in one hour of woe.

Fainter grew our hearts with anguish
  In that hour with peril rife,
When we saw the pilot flying,
  Terror-stricken for his life.

Then a man uprose before us—
  We had once despised his race—
But we saw a lofty purpose
  Lighting up his darkened face.

While the flames were madly roaring,
  With a courage grand and high,
Forth he rushed unto our rescue,
  Strong to suffer, brave to die.

Helplessly the host was drifting,
  Death was staring in each face,
When he grasped the fallen rudder,
  Took the pilot's vacant place.

Could he save us? Would he save us?
  All his hope of life give o'er?
Could he hold the fated vessel
  'Till she reached the nearer shore?

All our hopes and fears were centered
  'Round his strong, unfaltering hand;
If he failed us we must perish,
  Perish just in sight of land.

Breathlessly we watched and waited
  While the flames were raging fast;
Then our anguish changed to rapture—
  We were saved, yes, saved at last.

Never strains of sweetest music
  Brought to me more welcome sound
Than the grating of that steamer
  When her keel had touched the ground.

But our faithful martyr hero
　　Through a fiery pathway trod,
'Till he laid his valiant spirit
　　On the bosom of his God.

Fame has never crowned a hero
　　On the crimson fields of strife,
Greater, nobler, than that pilot
　　Yielding up for us his life.

THE DYING BONDMAN

Life was trembling, faintly trembling
On the bondman's latest breath,
And he felt the chilling pressure
Of the cold, hard hand of Death.

He had been an Afric chieftain,
Worn his manhood as a crown;
But upon the field of battle
Had been fiercely stricken down.

He had longed to gain his freedom,
Waited, watched and hoped in vain,
Till his life was slowly ebbing—
Almost broken was his chain.

By his bedside stood the master,
Gazing on the dying one,
Knowing by the dull grey shadows
That life's sands were almost run.

"Master," said the dying bondman,
"Home and friends I soon shall see;
But before I reach my country,
Master write that I am free;

"For the spirits of my fathers
Would shrink back from me in pride,
If I told them at our greeting
I a slave had lived and died;—

"Give to me the precious token,
That my kindred dead may see—
Master! write it, write it quickly!
Master! write that I am free!"

At his earnest plea the master
Wrote for him the glad release,
O'er his wan and wasted features
Flitted one sweet smile of peace.

Eagerly he grasped the writing;
"I am free!" at last he said.
Backward fell upon the pillow,
He was free among the dead.

A LITTLE CHILD SHALL LEAD THEM

Only a little scrap of blue
   Preserved with loving care,
But earth has not a brilliant hue
   To me more bright and fair.

Strong drink, like a raging demon,
   Laid on my heart his hand,
When my darling joined with others
   The Loyal Legion* band.

But mystic angels called away
   My loved and precious child,
And o'er life's dark and stormy way
   Swept waves of anguish wild.

* The Temperance Band

This badge of the Loyal Legion
    We placed upon her breast,
As she lay in her little coffin
    Taking her last sweet rest.

To wear that badge was a token
    She earnestly did crave,
So we laid it on her bosom
    To wear it in the grave.

Where sorrow would never reach her
    Nor harsh words smite her ear;
Nor her eyes in death dimmed slumber
    Would ever shed a tear.

"What means this badge?" said her father,
    Whom we had tried to save;
Who said, when we told her story,
    "Don't put it in the grave."

We took the badge from her bosom
    And laid it on a chair;
And men by drink deluded
    Knelt by that badge in prayer.

And vowed in that hour of sorrow
    From drink they would abstain;
And this little badge became the wedge
    Which broke their galling chain.

And lifted the gloomy shadows
    That overspread my life,
And flooding my home with gladness,
    Made me a happy wife.

And this is why this scrap of blue
    Is precious in my sight;
It changed my sad and gloomy home
    From darkness into light.

THE SPARROW'S FALL

Too frail to soar—a feeble thing—
It fell to earth with fluttering wing;
But God, who watches over all,
Beheld that little sparrow's fall.

'Twas not a bird with plumage gay,
Filling the air with its morning lay;
'Twas not an eagle bold and strong,
Borne on the tempest's wing along.

Only a brown and weesome thing,
With drooping head and listless wing;
It could not drift beyond His sight
Who marshals the spendid stars of night.

Its dying chirp fell on His ears,
Who tunes the music of the spheres,
Who hears the hungry lion's call,
And spreads a table for us all.

Its mission of song at last is done,
No more will it greet the rising sun;
That tiny bird has found a rest
More calm than its mother's downy breast.

Oh, restless heart, learn thou to trust
In God, so tender, strong and just;
In whose love and mercy everywhere
His humblest children have a share.

If in love He numbers ev'ry hair,
Whether the strands be dark or fair,
Shall we not learn to calmly rest,
Like children, on our Father's breast?

GOD BLESS OUR NATIVE LAND

God bless our native land,
  Land of the newly free,
Oh may she ever stand
  For truth and liberty.

God bless our native land,
  Where sleep our kindred dead,
Let peace at thy command
  Above their graves be shed.

God help our native land,
  Bring surcease to her strife,
And shower from thy hand
  A more abundant life.

God bless our native land,
  Her homes and children bless,
Oh may she ever stand
  For truth and righteousness.

DANDELIONS

Welcome children of the Spring,
  In your garbs of green and gold,
Lifting up your sun-crowned heads
  On the verdant plain and wold.

As a bright and joyous troop
  From the breast of earth ye came
Fair and lovely are your cheeks,
  With sun-kisses all aflame.

In the dusty streets and lanes,
  Where the lowly children play,
There as gentle friends ye smile,
  Making brighter life's highway.

Dewdrops and the morning sun,
    Weave your garments fair and bright,
And we welcome you to-day
    As the children of the light.

Children of the earth and sun,
    We are slow to understand
All the richness of the gifts
    Flowing from our Father's hand.

Were our visions clearer far,
    In this sun-dimmed world of ours,
Would we not more thankful be
    For the love that sends us flowers?

Welcome, early visitants,
    With your sun-crowned golden hair,
With your message to our hearts
    Of our Father's loving care.

HOME, SWEET HOME

Sharers of a common country,
    They had met in deadly strife;
Men who should have been as brothers
    Madly sought each other's life.

In the silence of the even,
    When the cannon's lips were dumb,
Thoughts of home and all its loved ones
    To the soldier's heart would come.

On the margin of a river,
    'Mid the evening's dews and damps,
Could be heard the sounds of music
    Rising from two hostile camps.

One was singing of its section
  Down in Dixie, Dixie's land,
And the other of the banner
  Waved so long from strand to strand.

In the land where Dixie's ensign
  Floated o'er the hopeful slave,
Rose the song that freedom's banner,
  Starry-lighted, long might wave.

From the fields of strife and carnage,
  Gentle thoughts began to roam,
And a tender strain of music
  Rose with words of "Home, Sweet Home.'

Then the hearts of strong men melted,
  For amid our grief and sin
Still remains that "touch of nature,"
  Telling us we all are kin.

In one grand but gentle chorus,
  Floating to the starry dome,
Came the words that brought them nearer,
  Words that told of "Home, Sweet Home."

For a while, all strife forgotten,
  They were only brothers then,
Joining in the sweet old chorus,
  Not as soldiers, but as men.

Men whose hearts would flow together,
  Though apart their feet might roam,
Found a tie they could not sever,
  In the mem'ry of each home.

Never may the steps of carnage
  Shake our land from shore to shore,
But may mother, home and Heaven,
  Be our watchwords evermore.

THE BUILDING

"Build me a house," said the Master,
  "But not on the shifting sand,
Mid the wreck and roar of tempests,
  A house that will firmly stand.

"I will bring thee windows of agates,
  And gates of carbuncles bright,
And thy fairest courts and portals
  Shall be filled with love and light.

"Thou shalt build with fadeless rubies,
  All fashioned around the throne,
A house that shall last forever,
  With Christ as the cornerstone.

"It shall be a royal mansion,
  A fair and beautiful thing,
It will be the presence-chamber
  Of thy Saviour, Lord and King.

"Thy house shall be bound with pinions
  To mansions of rest above,
But grace shall forge all the fetters
  With the links and cords of love.

"Thou shalt be free in this mansion
  From sorrow and pain of heart,
For the peace of God shall enter,
  And never again depart."

THE PURE IN HEART
SHALL SEE GOD

They shall see Him in the crimson flush
  Of morning's early light,

In the drapery of sunset,
    Around the couch of night.

When the clouds drop down their fatness,
    In the late and early rain,
They shall see His glorious footprints
    On valley, hill and plain.

They shall see Him when the cyclone
    Breathes terror through the land;
They shall see Him 'mid the murmurs
    Of zephyrs soft and bland.

They shall see Him when the lips of health,
    Breath vigor through each nerve,
When pestilence clasps hands with death,
    His purposes to serve.

They shall see Him when the trembling earth
    Is rocking to and fro;
They shall see Him in the order
    The seasons come and go.

They shall see Him when the storms of war
    Sweep wildly through the land;
When peace descends like gentle dew
    They still shall see His hand.

They shall see Him in the city
    Of gems and pearls of light,
They shall see Him in his beauty,
    And walk with Him in white.

To living founts their feet shall tend,
    And Christ shall be their guide,
Beloved of God, their rest shall be
    In safety by His side.

HE HAD NOT WHERE
TO LAY HIS HEAD

The conies had their hiding-place,
   The wily fox with stealthy tread
A covert found, but Christ, the Lord,
   Had not a place to lay his head.

The eagle had an eyrie home,
   The blithesome bird its quiet rest,
But not the humblest spot on earth
   Was by the Son of God possessed.

Princes and kings had palaces,
   With grandeur could adorn each tomb,
For Him who came with love and life,
   They had no home, they gave no room.

The hands whose touch sent thrills of joy
   Through nerves unstrung and palsied frame,
The feet that travelled for our need,
   Were nailed unto the cross of shame.

How dare I murmur at my lot,
   Or talk of sorrow, pain and loss,
When Christ was in a manger laid,
   And died in anguish on the cross.

That homeless one beheld beyond
   His lonely agonizing pain,
A love outflowing from His heart,
   That all the wandering world would gain.

GO WORK IN MY VINEYARD

Go work in my vineyard, said the Lord,
   And gather the bruised grain;

But the reapers had left the stubble bare,
    And I trod the soil in pain.

The fields of my Lord are wide and broad,
    He has pastures fair and green,
And vineyards that drink the golden light
    Which flows from the sun's bright sheen.

I heard the joy of the reaper's song,
    As they gathered golden grain;
Then wearily turned unto my task,
    With a lonely sense of pain.

Sadly I turned from the sun's fierce glare,
    And sought the quiet shade,
And over my dim and weary eyes
    Sleep's peaceful fingers strayed.

I dreamed I joined with a restless throng,
    Eager for pleasure and gain;
But ever and anon a stumbler fell,
    And uttered a cry of pain.

But the eager crowd still hurried on,
    Too busy to pause or heed,
When a voice rang sadly through my soul,
    You must staunch these wounds that bleed.

My hands were weak, but I reached them out
    To feebler ones than mine,
And over the shadows of my life
    Stole the light of a peace divine.

Oh! then my task was a sacred thing,
    How precious it grew in my eyes!
'Twas mine to gather the bruised grain
    For the "Lord of Paradise."

And when the reapers shall lay their grain
   On the floors of golden light,
I feel that mine with its broken sheaves
   Shall be precious in His sight.

Though thorns may often pierce my feet,
   And the shadows still abide,
The mists will vanish before His smile,
   There will be light at eventide.

RENEWAL OF STRENGTH

The prison-house in which I live
   Is falling to decay,
But God renews my spirit's strength,
   Within these walls of clay.

For me a dimness slowly creeps
   Around earth's fairest light,
But heaven grows clearer to my view,
   And fairer to my sight.

It may be earth's sweet harmonies
   Are duller to my ear,
But music from my Father's house
   Begins to float more near.

Then let the pillars of my home
   Crumble and fall away;
Lo, God's dear love within my soul
   Renews it day by day.

JAMIE'S PUZZLE

There was grief within our household
   Because of a vacant chair.

Our mother, so loved and precious,
    No longer was sitting there.

Our hearts grew heavy with sorrow,
    Our eyes with tears were blind,
And little Jamie was wondering,
    Why we were left behind.

We had told our little darling,
    Of the land of love and light,
Of the saints all crowned with glory,
    And enrobed in spotless white.

We said that our precious mother,
    Had gone to that land so fair,
To dwell with beautiful angels,
    And to be forever there.

But the child was sorely puzzled,
    Why dear grandmamma should go
To dwell in a stranger city,
    When her children loved her so.

But again the mystic angel
    Came with swift and silent tread,
And our sister, Jamie's mother,
    Was enrolled among the dead.

To us the mystery deepened,
    To Jamie it seemed more clear;
Grandma, he said, must be lonesome,
    And mamma has gone to her.

But the question lies unanswered
    In our little Jamie's mind,
Why she should go to our mother,
    And leave her children behind;

To dwell in that lovely city,
From all that was dear to part,
From children who loved to nestle
So closely around her heart.

Dear child, like you, we are puzzled,
With problems that still remain;
But think in the great hereafter
Their meaning will all be plain.

AN APPEAL TO MY COUNTRY WOMEN

You can sigh o'er the sad-eyed Armenian
Who weeps in her desolate home.
You can mourn o'er the exile of Russia
From kindred and friends doomed to roam.

You can pity the men who have woven
From passion and appetite chains
To coil with a terrible tension
Around their heartstrings and brains.

You can sorrow o'er little children
Disinherited from their birth,
The wee waifs and toddlers neglected,
Robbed of sunshine, music and mirth.

For beasts you have gentle compassion;
Your mercy and pity they share.
For the wretched, outcast and fallen
You have tenderness, love and care.

But hark! from our Southland are floating
Sobs of anguish, murmurs of pain,
And women heart-stricken are weeping
Over their tortured and their slain.

On their brows the sun has left traces;
    Shrink not from their sorrow in scorn.
When they entered the threshold of being
    The children of a King were born.

Each comes as a guest to the table
    The hands of our God has outspread,
To fountains that ever leap upward,
    To share in the soil we all tread.

When we plead for the wrecked and fallen,
    The exile from far-distant shores,
Remember that men are still wasting
    Life's crimson around our own doors.

Have ye not, oh, my favored sisters,
    Just a plea, a prayer or a tear,
For mothers who dwell 'neath the shadows
    Of agony, hatred and fear?

Men may tread down the poor and lowly,
    May crush them in anger and hate,
But surely the mills of God's justice
    Will grind out the grist of their fate.

Oh, people sin-laden and guilty,
    So lusty and proud in your prime,
The sharp sickles of God's retribution
    Will gather your harvest of crime.

Weep not, oh my well-sheltered sisters,
    Weep not for the Negro alone,
But weep for your sons who must gather
    The crops which their fathers have sown.

Go read on the tombstones of nations
    Of chieftains who masterful trod,
The sentence which time has engraven,
    That they had forgotten their God.

'Tis the judgment of God that men reap
   The tares which in madness they sow,
Sorrow follows the footsteps of crime,
   And Sin is the consort of Woe.

THE LOST BELLS

Year after year the artist wrought
   With earnest, loving care,
The music flooding all his soul
   To pour upon the air.

For this no metal was too rare,
   He counted not the cost;
Nor deemed the years in which he toiled
   As labor vainly lost.

When morning flushed with crimson light
   The golden gates of day,
He longed to fill the air with chimes
   Sweet as a matin's lay.

And when the sun was sinking low
   Within the distant West,
He gladly heard the bells he wrought
   Herald the hour of rest.

The music of a thousand harps
   Could never be so dear
As when those solemn chants and thrills
   Fell on his list'ning ear.

He poured his soul into their chimes,
   And felt his toil repaid;
He called them children of his soul,
   His home a'near them made.

But evil days came on apace,
  War spread his banner wide,
And from his village snatched away
  The artist's love and pride.

At dewy morn and stilly eve
  The chimes no more he heard;
With dull and restless agony
  His spirit's depths was stirred.

A weary longing filled his soul,
  It bound him like a spell;
He left his home to seek the chimes—
  The chimes he loved so well.

Where lofty fanes in grandeur rose,
  Upon his ear there fell
No music like the long lost chimes
  Of his beloved bell.

And thus he wandered year by year.
  Touched by the hand of time,
Seeking to hear with anxious heart
  Each well remembered chime.

And to that worn and weary heart
  There came a glad surcease;
He heard again the dear old chimes,
  And smiled and uttered peace.

"The chimes! the chimes!" the old man cried,
  "I hear the tones at last";
A sudden rapture filled his heart,
  And all his cares were past.

Yes, peace had come with death's sweet calm,
  His journeying was o'er,
The weary, restless wanderer
  Had reached the restful shore.

It may be that we meet again,
  Enfolded in the air,
The dear old chimes beside the gates
  Where all is bright and fair;

That he who crossed and bowed his head
  When Angelus was sung
In clearer light touched golden harps
  By angel fingers strung.

"DO NOT CHEER, MEN ARE DYING,"
SAID CAPT. PHILLIPS,
IN THE SPANISH-AMERICAN WAR

Do not cheer, for men are dying
  From their distant homes in pain;
And the restless sea is darkened
  By a flood of crimson rain.

Do not cheer, for anxious mothers
  Wait and watch in lonely dread;
Vainly waiting for the footsteps
  Never more their paths to tread.

Do not cheer, while little children
  Gather round the widowed wife,
Wondering why an unknown people
  Sought their own dear father's life.

Do not cheer, for aged fathers
  Bend above their stoves and weep,
While the ocean sings the requiem
  Where their fallen children sleep.

Do not cheer, for lips are paling
  On which lay the mother's kiss;

'Mid the dreadful roar of battle
    How that mother's hand they miss!

Do not cheer, once joyous maidens,
    Who the mazy dance did tread,
Bow their heads in bitter anguish,
    Mourning o'er their cherished dead.

Do not cheer while maid and matron
    In this strife must bear a part;
While the blow that strikes a soldier
    Reaches to some woman's heart.

Do not cheer till arbitration
    O'er the nations holds its sway,
And the century now closing
    Ushers in a brighter day.

Do not cheer until each nation
    Sheathes the sword and blunts the spear,
And we sing aloud for gladness;
    Lo, the reign of Christ is here.

And the banners of destruction
    From the battlefield are furled,
And the peace of God descending
    Rests upon a restless world.

THE BURDENS OF ALL

We may sigh o'er the heavy burdens
    Of the black, the brown and white;
But if we all clasped hands together
    The burdens would be more light.
How to solve life's saddest problems,
    Its weariness, want and woe,
Was answered by One who suffered
    In Palestine long ago.

He gave from his heart this precept,
   To ease the burdens of men,
"As ye would that others do to you
   Do ye even so to them."
Life's heavy, wearisome burdens
   Will change to a gracious trust
When men shall learn in the light of God
   To be merciful and just.

Where war has sharpened his weapons,
   And slavery masterful had,
Let white and black and brown unite
   To build the kingdom of God.
And never attempt in madness
   To build a kingdom or state,
Through greed of gold or lust of power,
   On the crumbling stones of hate.

The burdens will always be heavy,
   The sunshine fade into night,
Till mercy and justice shall cement
   The black, the brown and the white.
And earth shall answer with gladness,
   The herald angel's refrain,
When "Peace on earth, good will to men"
   Was the burden of their strain.

A FAIRER HOPE,
A BRIGHTER MORN

From the peaceful heights of a higher life
I heard your maddening cry of strife;
It quivered with anguish, wrath and pain,
Like a demon struggling with his chain.

A chain of evil, heavy and strong,
Rusted with ages of fearful wrong,
Encrusted with blood and burning tears,
The chain I had worn and dragged for years.

It clasped my limbs, but it bound your heart,
And formed of your life a fearful part;
You sowed the wind, but could not control
The tempest wild of a guilty soul.

You saw me stand with my broken chain
Forged in the furnace of fiery pain,
You saw my children around me stand
Lovingly clasping my unbound hand.

But you remembered my blood and tears
'Mid the weary wasting flight of years,
You thought of the rice swamps, lone and dank,
When my heart in hopeless anguish sank.

You thought of your fields with harvest white,
Where I toiled in pain from morn till night;
You thought of the days you bought and sold
The children I loved, for paltry gold.

You thought of our shrieks that rent the air—
Our mourns of anguish and deep despair;
With chattering teeth and paling face,
You thought of your nation's deep disgrace.

You wove from your fears a fearful fate
To spring from your seeds of scorn and hate;
You imagined the saddest, wildest thing,
That time, with revenges fierce, could bring.

The cry you thought from a Voodo breast
Was the echo of your soul's unrest;
When thoughts too sad for fruitless tears
Loomed like the ghosts of avenging years.

Oh prophet of evil, could not your voice
In our new hopes and freedom rejoice?
'Mid the light which streams around our way
Was there naught to see but an evil day?

Nothing but vengeance, wrath and hate,
And the serpent coils of an evil fate—
A fate that shall crush and drag you down;
A doom that shall press like an iron crown?

A fate that shall crisp and curl your hair
And darken your faces now as fair,
And send through your veins like a poisoned flood
The hated stream of the Negro's blood?

A fate to madden the heart and brain
You've peopled with phantoms of dread and pain,
And fancies wild of your daughter's shriek
With Congo kisses upon her cheek?

Beyond the mist of your gloomy fears,
I see the promise of brighter years,
Through the dark I see their golden hem
And my heart gives out its glad amen.

The banner of Christ was your sacred trust,
But you trailed that banner in the dust,
And mockingly told us amid our pain
The hand of your God had forged our chain.

We stumbled and groped through the dreary night
Till our fingers touched God's robe of light;
And we knew he heard, from his lofty throne,
Our saddest cries and faintest moan.

The cross you have covered with sin and shame
We'll bear aloft in Christ's holy name.
Oh, never again may its folds be furled
While sorrow and sin enshroud our world!

God, to whose fingers thrills each heart beat,
Has not sent us to walk with aimless feet,
To cower and couch with bated breath
From margins of life to shores of death.

Higher and better than hate for hate,
Like the scorpion fangs that desolate,
Is the hope of a brighter, fairer morn
And a peace and love that shall yet be born;

When the Negro shall hold an honored place,
The friend and helper of every race;
His mission to build and not destroy,
And gladden the world with love and joy.

BE ACTIVE

Onward, onward, sons of freedom,
    In the great and glorious strife;
You've a high and holy mission
    On the battle field of life.

See oppression's feet of iron
    Grinds a brother to the ground,
And from bleeding heart and bosom
    Gapeth many a fearful wound.

Sit not down with idle pity
    Gazing on his mighty wrong,
Hurl the bloated tyrant from him
    Say, my brother, oh be strong!

See that sad despairing mother
    Clasp her burning brow in pain,
Lay your hands upon her fetters
    Rend, oh! rend, her galling chain!

Here's a pale and trembling maiden,
  Brutal arms around her thrown,
Christian father, save oh! save her
  By the love you bear your own!

Yearly lay a hundred thousand
  Newborn babes on Moloch's shrine,
Crush these gory reeking altars;
  Christian, let this work be thine.

Where the southern roses blossom,
  Weary lives go out in pain,
Dragging to death's shadowy portals
  Slavery's heavy galling chain.

Men of every clime and nation,
  Every faith, and sect, and creed,
Lay aside your idle jangling,
  Come and staunch the wounds that bleed.

On my people's blighted bosom
  Mountain weights of sorrow lay,
Stop not now to ask the question
  Who shall roll the stone away.

Set at work the moral forces
  That are yours of church and state,
Teach them how to war and battle
  'Gainst oppression, wrong, and hate.

Oh! be faithful! O, be valiant!
  Trusting not in human might,
Know that in the darkest conflict
  God is on the side of right.

"BEHOLD THE LILIES!"

Behold the lilies of the field
    How beautiful and fair;
Their fragrance as a breath of heaven
    Refreshes all the air.

No sordid labors bow them down,
    Nor dull depressing care;
They only tell of God's great love,
    And that is everywhere.

The wings of morning are too slow
    To bear us from His sight;
The midnight has no shadows deep
    To hide from us His light.

If not a sparrow falls to earth
    Unnoticed by His eye,
Will He, our Father and our Friend
    Unheeded pass us by?

Shall we not learn from fading flowers—
    Frail children of the dust—
To lay our cares before His throne,
    And in his mercy trust?

There's not a care that weights us down,
    No blinding tears that fall,
Nor sorrow piercing to the heart
    But he beholds them all;

And offers us with tender love,
    Mid dangers and alarms,
A refuge for our souls within
    His everlasting arms.

TO BISHOP PAYNE

Written for the special celebration of the fortieth anniversary of Daniel A. Payne as bishop of the A. M. E. Church, 1892.

The prison house in which you dwell,
    Is falling to decay.
May God renew thy spirit's youth,
    Within those walls of clay.

And while a dimness slowly creeps
    Around Earth's fairest light,
May heaven grow clearer to your view,
    And fairer to thy sight.

And when Earth's sweetest harmonies
    Grow duller to your ear,
May music from your father's house
    Begin to float more near.

Then let the pillars of your home
    Crumble and fall away.
So God's dear love within thy soul
    Renews it day by day.

Until life's toil and pain are o'er,
    Its sorrow and its night.
And on thy raptured gaze shall burst
    The beatific sight.

With saints redeemed and martyrs crowned,
    And loved ones mayest thou meet;
And rest with them thy crown of life,
    At our Redeemer's feet.

"GONE TO GOD"

Finished now the weary throbbing,
  Of a bosom calmed to rest;
Laid aside the heavy sorrows,
  That for years upon it prest.

All the thirst for pure affection,
  All the hunger of the heart;
All the vain and tearful cryings,
  All forever now depart.

Clasp the pale and faded fingers,
  O'er the cold and lifeless form;
They shall never shrink and shiver,
  Homeless in the dark and storm.

Press the death-weights calmly, gently,
  O'er the eyelids in their sleep;
Tears shall never tremble from them,
  They shall never wake to weep.

Close the silent lips together,
  Lips once parted with a sigh;
Through their sealed, moveless portals,
  Ne'er shall float a bitter cry.

Bring no bright and blooming flowers,
  Let no mournful tears be shed,
Funeral flowers, tears of sorrow,
  They are for the cherished dead.

She has been a lonely wanderer,
  Drifting on the world's highway;
Grasping with her woman's nature,
  Feeble reeds to be her stay.

God is witness to the anguish,
   Of a heart that's all alone;
Floating blindly on life's current,
   Only bound unto His throne.

But o'er such, Death's solemn angel,
   Broodeth with a sheltering wing;
Till the hopeless hand's grown weary,
   Cease around earth's toys to cling.

Then kind hands will clasp them gently,
   On the still, unaching breast;
Softly treading by, they'll whisper,
   Of the lone one gone to rest.

IN COMMEMORATION OF THE CENTENNIAL OF THE A. M. E. CHURCH

A little seed in weakness sown,
   Fell in the desert dust—
In Allen's hand that seed became
   A sacred, precious trust.

Around it swept the arid airs
   Of prejudice and hate,
And heaven's bright dew upon it fell,
   And God watched o'er its fate.

And Faith and Sacrifice, like rain,
   Fell softly at its base,
Until amid the elder trees,
   A scion took its place.

Now where the broad Atlantic breaks
    In sprays of crested foam
Or, sobbing near our sunset mounts,
    Is heard Pacific's moan—

From shore to shore its branches spread
    From snow-clad hills of Maine
To where, against our coral reefs,
    The wild waves dash in vain.

Its roots have run beyond the sea
    To Hayti's sunny strand,
And spread its branches far away
    In Africa's distant land.

May every fruit of God's rich grace
    This tree for men afford,
And flourish 'mid the vales of life
    A planting of the Lord.

Beneath its shade may weary hearts
    Find shelter, love and rest,
And with a glad surrender make
    Our earth more bright and blest.

May He who prunes and bears away
    The branch He cannot own
Help this to be a fruitful tree
    To plant around His throne.

LESSONS OF THE STREET

Walking through life's dusty highways,
    Mid the tramp of hurrying feet,
We may gather such instruction,
    From the lessons 'of the street'.

Now a beggar sues for succor—
   Nay, repress that look of pride!
'Neath that wrecked and shattered body
   Doth a human soul reside.

Here's a brow that seems to tell you,
   'I am prematurely old;
I have spent my youthful vigor
   In an eager search for gold'.

On the cheek of yon pale student
   Is a divorcement most unkind—
'Tis the cruel separation
   Of his body from his mind.

Here a painted child of shame
   Flaunts in costly robes of sin,
With a reckless mirth that cannot
   Hide the smoldering fires within.

And here's a face so calm and mild,
   Mid the restless din and strife;
It seems to say in every line,
   'I'm aiming for a higher life'.

Just then I caught a mournful glance,
   As on the human river rushed,
A harrowing look which plainly said,
   'The music of my life is hushed'.

Look on that face, so deathly pale,
   Its bloom and flush forever fled;
I started, for it seemed to bear
   A message to the silent dead.

Thus hurries on the stream of life,
   To empty where Death's waters meet;
We pass along, we pass away—
   Thus end the lessons of the street.

A POEM

Composed for the reception tendered the Reverend Henry
L. Phillips and wife in celebration of their return from West
Indies in 1902 and of his twenty-five years of service as rector
of the Church of the Crucifixion, Philadelphia.

Over the foaming ocean,
    Over the restless sea;
Back to thy field of labor,
    We are waiting to welcome thee.

Back from the land of flowers,
    Kissed by the ardent sun;
With thy brightest, gladdest welcome,
    Thy people here are come.

In the long, long Lenten season,
    Ere thy journeyings were o'er;
We will not forget the lessons,
    Taught us by our Brother More.

In the work thou placed before,
    He has laid his earnest heart;
So tonight within thy welcome
    He must surely take a part.

Youth and maiden here will greet thee,
    Who were not confirmed before;
Greet thee here tonight as pastor,
    By the work of Brother More.

With the consort of thy bosom,
    As down the stream of life ye glide;
May the love of God surround you
    With His light at eventide.

In the years of early manhood,
   On thy brow the dews of youth,
Thou gaves't to a needed people
   Many words of love and truth.

Now we welcome thee, dear Father,
   As one who points the way
Amid earth's pomps and vanities
   To Heaven's brighter day.

May rich and copious blessing
   Upon thy life descend,
As we greet thee with a welcome,
   Our Father and our friend.

Where sin clasps hand with sorrow,
   May we thy flock be found;
As followers of the Master,
   Who in his love abound.

To strive by high endeavor
   To make the world more bright;
To change life's dull and rugged paths,
   To lines of living light.

With hearts of glad surrender,
   Not seeking wealth or fame;
O Guide and Shepherd teach us
   To live in Jesus' name.

With peace and joy and comfort,
   May all thy life be blessed;
And angels welcome thee at last
   Within the gates of rest.

With all the saints and martyrs,
   Who tried with pain and might;
With bleeding feet the thorny paths,
   Now luminous with light.

Like a holy Benediction,
    Thy presence may it be;
Till in the Holy City
    Thy flock shall welcome thee.

THE SOUL

Bring forth the balance, let the weight be gold!
We'd know the worth of a deathless soul;
Bring rubies and gems from every mine,
With the wealth of ocean, land and clime.

Bring the joys of the green, green earth,
Its playful smiles and careless mirth;
The dews of youth and flushes of health—
Bring! Oh, bring! the wide world's wealth.

Bring the rich, rare pearls of thought
From the depths of knowledge brought,
All that human ken may know,
Searching earth and heaven o'er.

Bring the fairest rolls of fame—
Rolls unwritten with a deed of shame;
Honor's guerdon, victory's crown,
Robes of pride, wreaths of renown.

We've brought the wealth of ev'ry mine,
We've ransacked ocean, land and clime,
And caught the joyous smiles away,
From the prattling babe to the sire gray.

We've wrought the names of the noble dead,
With those who in their footsteps tread,
Here are wreaths of pride and gems of thought,
From the battle-field and study brought.

Heap high the gems, pile up the gold,
For heavy's the weight of a deathless soul—
Make room for all the wealth of earth,
Its honors, joys, and careless mirth.

Leave me a niche for the rolls of fame—
Oh, precious, indeed, is a spotless name,
For the robes, the wreaths, and gems of thought,
Let an empty space in the scales be sought.

With care we've adjusted balance and scale,
Futile our efforts we've seen them fail;
Lighter than dust is the wealth of the earth,
Weighted in the scales with immortal worth.

Could we drag the sun from his golden car,
To lay in this balance with ev'ry star,
'Twould darken the day and obscure the night—
But the weight of the balance would still be light.

TO THE UNION SAVERS OF CLEVELAND

Men of Cleveland, had a vulture
    Sought a timid dove for prey,
Would you not, with human pity,
    Drive the gory bird away?

Had you seen a feeble lambkin,
    Shrinking from a wolf so bold,
Would ye not to shield the trembler,
    In your arms have made its fold?

But when she, a hunted sister,
    Stretched her hands that ye might save,
Colder far than Zembla's regions
    Was the answer that ye gave.

On the Union's bloody altar,
   Was your hapless victim laid;
Mercy, truth and justice shuddered,
   But your hands would give no aid.

And ye sent her back to torture,
   Robbed of freedom and of right.
Thrust the wretched, captive stranger,
   Back to slavery's gloomy night.

Back where brutal men may trample,
   On her honor and her fame;
And unto her lips so dusky,
   Press the cup of woe and shame.

There is blood upon your city,
   Dark and dismal is the strain;
And your hands would fail to cleanse it,
   Though Lake Erie ye should drain.

There's a curse upon your Union,
   Fearful sounds are in the air;
As if thunderbolts were framing
   Answers to the bondsman's prayer.

Ye may offer human victims,
   Like the heathen priests of old;
And may barter manly honor
   For the Union and for gold.

But ye can not stay the whirlwind,
   When the storm begins to break;
And your God doth rise in judgment,
   For the poor and needy's sake.

And, your sin-cursed, guilty Union
   Shall be shaken to its base,
Till ye learn that simple justice,
   Is the right of every race.

THE VISION OF
THE CZAR OF RUSSIA

To the Czar of all the Russians
    Came a vision bright and fair,
The joy of unburdened millions,
    Floating gladly on the air.

The laughter and songs of children,
    Of maidens, so gay and bright,
Of mothers who never would tremble,
    Where warfare and carnage blight.

Instead of the tramp of armies,
    Was patter of little feet;
The blare of bugles and trumpets,
    Had melted in music sweet.

The harvests had ceased to ripen,
    On fields that were drenched with blood;
The seas no more were ensanguined
    With an awful crimson flood.

The peaceful pavements no longer
    Re-echoed the martial tread;
And over the ransomed nations
    The banner of love was spread.

The streams tripped lightly seaward,
    Unfreighted with human gore;
The valleys and hills were brightened,
    And shuddered with strife no more.

There were homes where peace and plenty
    Around happy hearths did smile;
And the touch of baby fingers,
    Could sorrow and care beguile.

The cannon had ceased its bristling,
　　Its mission of death was o'er;
And the world so weary of carnage,
　　Learned the art of war was no more.

And Earth, once so sorrow laden,
　　Grew daily more fair and bright;
Till peace our globe had unfolded,
　　And millions walked in its light.

'Twas a bright and beautiful vision,
　　Of nations disarmed and free;
As to heaven across the chorus
　　Of the world's first jubilee.

How long shall the vision tarry?
　　How long shall the hours delay,
Till war shrinks our saddened Earth,
　　As the darkness shrinks from day?

Till barracks shall change to churches,
　　The prison become a school;
And over the hearts and homes of men,
　　The peace of our God shall rule?

And Earth, like a barque, storm riven,
　　The sport of tempest and tide;
Shall find rest and a haven
　　The heart of the Crucified.

FOR THE TWENTY-FIFTH ANNIVERSARY OF THE HOME FOR AGED AND INFIRM COLORED PERSONS

We come, but not to celebrate
Amid the flight and whirl of years,

The deeds of heroes, on whose brows
Are laurels, drenched with blood and tears.

Nor yet to tell of wondrous deeds
Performed on fields of bloodless strife;
But of the lonely precious things,
That bless and beautify our life.

And from the annals of the poor
We would unfold a shining page;
And tell of kindly hands that smoothed
The rugged path of faltering age.

To shelter those who long have borne
Life's chilling storms and searching heat,
In restful homes, with love alight
What charity more pure and sweet?

But not beneath this spacious Home
Was laid the first foundation stone,
But in the hearts that learned to feel
For woman stricken, old and lone.

To Hall and Truman, Still and Laing
Was given power to aid and bless;
And, faithful to her sacred charge,
Constant, and helping, stood Ann Jess.

May Sarah Pennock, whose kind hand
Has often brought the "Home" relief
Feel life replete with God's great peace;
Find light in darkness, joy in grief.

Custodian of the Generous purse
May Israel Johnson long remain—
And reach at last the happy land,
Where faithful service meets its gain.

And join again departed forms
Of wife and sister passed before;

Who gave their treasure to the Lord,
By generous gifts unto His poor.

And some who met with us erewhile,
Have passed unto the other side;
Like precious fragrance, may their deeds
Within our heart of hearts abide.

Year after year, within these walls,
Did Dillwyn Parrish faithful stand;
Til He "Who gives his loved ones sleep"
Released, in death, his helpful hand.

Of those who scattered flowers fair
Around the verge of parting life,
We would record with grateful words,
The names of Stephen Smith and wife.

Whose hands, enriched with golden store,
Gave of their wealth to build this "Home,'
And changed a narrow domicile
Into a grand and stately dome.

Oh! When our earthly homes shall fail
And vanish from our fading sight
May friends and patrons meet again
In God's fair halls of love and light.

Where homeless ones shall never weep,
Nor weary aged wanderers roam;
But walk amid the golden streets
Secure within our Father's home.

APPENDIX

Prepared by Susanne Dietzel

A CHRONOLOGICAL LIST OF FRANCES ELLEN WATKINS HARPER'S POETRY

Eliza Harris (1853)*
The Syrophenician Woman (1854)
The Slave Mother (1854)
Bible Defence of Slavery (1854)
Ethiopia (1854)
The Drunkard's Child (1854)
The Slave Auction (1854)
The Revel (1854)
That Blessed Hope (1854)
The Dying Christian (1854)
Report (1854)
Advice to the Girls (1854)
Saved by Faith (1854)
Died of Starvation (1854)
A Mother's Heroism (1854)
The Fugitive's Wife (1854)
The Contrast (1854)
The Prodigal's Return (1854)
Eva's Farewell (1854)
Be Active (1856)
Lessons of the Street (1858)
"Gone To God" (1859)
To the Union Savers of Cleveland (1861)

*Originally published in *Frederick Douglass' Paper*, December 23, 1853, included in *Poems on Miscellaneous Subjects* (1854).

219

Bury Me in a Free Land (1864)*
Moses (1869)
Lines to Hon. Thaddeus Stevens (1871)
An Appeal to the American People (1871)
Truth (1871)
Death of the Old Sea King (1871)
Let the Light Enter! (1871)
Youth in Heaven (1871)
Death of Zombi (1871)
Lines to Charles Sumner (1871)
"Sir, We Would See Jesus" (1871)
The Bride of Death (1871)
Thank God for Little Children (1871)
The Dying Fugitive (1871)
The Freedom Bell (1871)
Mary at the Feet of Christ (1871)
The Mother's Blessing (1871)
Vashti (1871)
The Change (1871)
The Dying Mother (1871)
Words for the Hour (1871)
President Lincoln's Proclamation of Freedom (1871)
To a Babe Smiling in Her Sleep (1871)
The Artist (1871)
Jesus (1871)
Fifteenth Amendment (1871)
Retribution (1871)
The Sin of Achan (1871)
Lines to Miles O'Reiley (1871)
The Little Builders (1871)
The Dying Child to Her Blind Father (1871)
Light in Darkness (1871)

*Originally published in the *Liberator* (1864), then included in *Poems* (1871).

Our English Friends (1872)
Aunt Chloe (1872)
   The Deliverance (1872)
   Aunt Chloe's Politics (1872)
   Learning to Read (1872)
   Church Building (1872)
   The Reunion (1872)
I Thirst (1872)
The Dying Queen (1872)
The Tennessee Hero (1874)
Free Labor (1874)
Lines (1874)
The Dismissal of Tyng (1874)
The Slave Mother, a Tale of the Ohio (1874)
Rizpah, the Daughter of Ai (1874)
Ruth and Naomi (1874)
The Jewish Grandfather's Story (1887/88)
Out in the Cold (1887/88)
Save the Boys (1887/88)
Nothing and Something (1887/88)
Wanderer's Return (1887/88)
Fishers of Men (1887/88)
Signing the Pledge (1887/88)
For the Twenty-Fifth Anniversary of The Home for Aged and
   Infirm Colored Persons (1889)
In Commemoration of the Centennial of the A. M. E. Church
   (1891)
To Bishop Payne (1892)
The Martyr of Alabama (1894)
The Night of Death (1894)
Mother's Treasures (1894)
The Refiner's Gold (1894)
A Story of the Rebellion (1894)
Burial of Sarah (1894)
Going East (1894)

The Hermit's Sacrifice (1894)
Songs for the People (1894)
An Appeal to My Country Women (1894)
Then and Now (1894)
Maceo (1894)
Only a Word (1894)
My Mother's Kiss (1895)
A Grain of Sand (1895)
The Crocuses (1895)
The Present Age (1895)
Dedication Poem (1895)
A Double Standard (1895)
Our Hero (1895)
The Dying Bondman (1895)
A Little Child Shall Lead Them (1895)
The Sparrow's Fall (1895)
God Bless Our Native Land (1895)
Dandelions (1895)
The Building (1895)
Home, Sweet Home (1895)
The Pure in Heart Shall See God (1895)
He Had Not Where to Lay His Head (1895)
Go Work in My Vineyard (1895)
Renewal of Strength (1895)
Jamie's Puzzle (1895)
The Vision of the Czar of Russia (1899)
The Lost Bells (1900)
"Do Not Cheer, Men are Dying," Said Capt. Phillips, in the
    Spanish-American War (1900)
The Burdens of All (1900)
"Behold the Lilies!" (1900)
The Ragged Stocking (1901)
The Fatal Pledge (1901)
Christ's Entry into Jerusalem (1901)
The Resurrection of Jesus (1901)

Simon's Countrymen (1901)
Deliverance (1901)
Simon's Feast (1901)
A Poem (1929)
The Soul (no date)
A Fairer Hope, A Brighter Morn (no date)

HARPER'S POETRY
BY PUBLISHED VOLUME*

POEMS ON MISCELLANEOUS SUBJECTS. Second Edition.
Boston: J. B. Yerrinton & Son, 1854.
  The Syrophenician Woman
  The Slave Mother
  Bible Defence of Slavery
  Eliza Harris
  Ethiopia
  The Drunkard's Child
  The Slave Auction
  The Revel
  That Blessed Hope
  The Dying Christian
  Report
  Advice to the Girls
  Saved by Faith
  Died of Starvation
  A Mother's Heroism
  The Fugitive's Wife
  The Contrast
  The Prodigal's Return
  Eva's Farewell
  Notes: The following prose pieces appear in this volume under

* This bibliography only lists volumes that have been viewed by the editor.

the heading of *Miscellaneous Writings:* "Christianity," "The Bible," and "The Colored People in America."

MOSES: A STORY OF THE NILE. Second Edition.
Philadelphia: Merrihew & Son, 1869.
  Moses
  Notes: Daniel lists an edition of *Moses: A Story of the Nile* which contains some of the poems published in the 1901 edition of *Idylls of the Bible*. Contains a prose piece "The Mission of Flowers" on pages 44–47.

POEMS ON MISCELLANEOUS SUBJECTS. 20th Edition.
Philadelphia: Merrihew & Son, 1874. Same as 1857 edition.
  The Tennessee Hero
  Free Labor
  Lines
  The Dismissal of Tyng
  The Slave Mother, a Tale of the Ohio
  Rizpah, the Daughter of Ai
  Ruth and Naomi
  Notes: The contents of the 1854 edition of *Poems on Miscellaneous Subjects* precede the poems listed here.
    The following prose pieces appear in this volume under the heading *Miscellaneous Writings:* "Christianity," "The Colored People of America," and "Breathing the Air of Freedom."

POEMS
Philadelphia: Merrihew & Son, 1871. Library of Congress has copy with 1876 cover (Providence: Crawford & Greene) and 1871 title page. The Moorland-Spingarn Collection, Howard University, has an 1880 cover (Crawford & Greene) and 1871 title page.
  Lines to Hon. Thaddeus Stevens
  An Appeal to the American People
  Truth
  Death of the Old Sea King

Let the Light Enter!
Youth in Heaven
Death of Zombi
Lines to Charles Sumner
"Sir, We Would See Jesus"
The Bride of Death
Thank God for Little Children
The Dying Fugitive
Bury Me in a Free Land
The Freedom Bell
Mary at the Feet of Christ
The Mother's Blessing
Vashti
The Change
The Dying Mother
Words for the Hour
President Lincoln's Proclamation of Freedom
To a Babe Smiling in Her Sleep
The Artist
Jesus
Fifteenth Amendment
Retribution
The Sin of Achan
Lines to Miles O'Reiley
The Little Builders
The Dying Child to Her Blind Father
Light in Darkness

SKETCHES OF SOUTHERN LIFE
Philadelphia: Ferguson Bros., 1887; Merrihew & Son, 1888.
Copyright 1872.
    Aunt Chloe
        The Deliverance
        Aunt Chloe's Politics
        Learning to Read

Notes: For the 1872 edition of *Sketches of Southern Life*, Daniel lists "Our English Friends" as the first poem. The poems beginning with "The Jewish Grandfather's Story" and ending with "Signing the Pledge" appear in the 1887 and 1888 editions.

ATLANTA OFFERING: POEMS
Philadelphia: 1006 Bainbridge Street, 1895.
For a complete listing of the poems included in this volume, see the 1896 edition of *Poems* listed below. *Atlanta Offering* has all but "Let the Light Enter!" and "An Appeal to My Country Women."

POEMS
Philadelphia: 1006 Bainbridge Street, 1896.

The Sparrow's Fall
God Bless Our Native Land
Dandelions
The Building
Home, Sweet Home
The Pure in Heart Shall See God
He Had Not Where to Lay His Head
Go Work in My Vineyard
Renewal of Strength
Jamie's Puzzle
Truth
Death of the Old Sea King
Save the Boys
Nothing and Something
Vashti
Thank God For Little Children
The Martyr of Alabama
The Night of Death
Mother's Treasures
The Refiner's Gold
A Story of the Rebellion
Burial of Sarah
Going East
The Hermit's Sacrifice
Songs for the People
Let the Light Enter!
An Appeal to My Country Women

POEMS
Philadelphia: 1006 Bainbridge Street, 1898.
The same as 1896 edition of *Poems*.

POEMS
Philadelphia: 1006 Bainbridge Street, 1900.
This is the same as the 1896 edition of *Poems*. This volume contains

additional poems which are not listed in the Table of Contents. Three of these poems were not previously published; they are:

The Lost Bells

"Do Not Cheer, Men Are Dying," Said Capt. Phillips, in the Spanish-American War

The Burdens of All

The Poems "Then and Now," "Maceo," and "Only A Word" originally appear in the collection *The Martyr of Alabama* but were not included in *Atlanta Offering*, a compilation of *The Martyr of Alabama*, and *The Sparrow's Fall*. They are included in this 1900 edition of *Poems* for the first time, although they also are not listed in the Table of Contents.

IDYLLS OF THE BIBLE
Philadelphia: 1006 Bainbridge Street, 1901.

The Ragged Stocking
The Fatal Pledge
Christ's Entry into Jerusalem
The Resurrection of Jesus
Simon's Countrymen
Deliverance
Simon's Feast

THE SPARROW'S FALL AND OTHER POEMS
No date

My Mother's Kiss
A Grain of Sand
The Crocuses
The Present Age
Dedication Poem
A Double Standard
Our Hero
A Little Child Shall Lead Them
The Sparrow's Fall

Other Sources*

Be Active. *Frederick Douglass' Paper*, January 11, 1856.

"Behold The Lilies!" *A. M. E. Church Review* XVI (1900).

To Bishop Payne. *Journal of the 20th Session and 19th Quadrennial Session of the Central Conference of the African Methodist Episcopal Church . . . Bethel Church, Philadelphia, Pennsylvania, May 2, 1892*, p. 61.

A Fairer Hope, A Brighter Morn. Published in *Light Beyond Darkness* (n.d.). A copy of this volume could not be located by the editor.

For the Twenty-Fifth Anniversary of The Home for Aged and Infirm Colored Persons. Published in the Annual Report of the Home for the Aged and Infirm Colored People, 1889.

"Gone To God." *Anglo-African* 1 (1859), 123.

In Commemoration of the Centennial of the A. M. E. Church. Published in *A. M. E. Church Review* VII (1891), 292, and in Benjamin W. Arnett, ed. *The Centennial Budget, Containing Account of the Celebration* (November 1887), pp. 549–50.

Lessons of the Street. *Liberator*, May 14, 1858.

A Poem. *Golden Jubilee of Henry Laird Phillips*. George F. Bragg, ed. c. 1929.

The Soul. In Payne, Daniel A. *History of the A. M. E. Church*, Nashville, TN: Publishing House of the A. M. E. Sunday-school Union, 1891, p. 302.

To the Union Savers of Cleveland. *Liberator* XXX (1861), 40; and William Still, *The Underground Railroad*, pp. 764–65.

---

* The citations are taken from Theodora Williams Daniel, "The Poems of Frances E. W. Harper, Edited with a Biographical and Critical Introduction, and Bibliography" (Master's Thesis, Howard University, 1937), and Leslie J. Pollard, "Frances Harper and the Old People: Two Recently Discovered Poems," *The Griot* 4 (Summer/Winter 1985): 52–56.

The Vision of the Czar of Russia. *A. M. E. Church Review* XVI (1899), 140–41.

LIBRARY HOLDINGS

Schomburg Collection

Atlanta Offering: Poems. Philadelphia: Ferguson, 1895.

Idylls of the Bible. Philadelphia, 1901.

Moses: A Story of the Nile. Philadelphia: Merrihew & Son, 1869.

Moses: A Story of the Nile. Second Edition. Philadelphia: Merrihew & Son, 1869.

Moses: A Story of the Nile. Second Edition. Philadelphia: 1006 Bainbridge Street, 1889.

Poems. Philadelphia: Ferguson, 1900, c. 1895.

Poems on Miscellaneous Subjects. Boston: J. B. Yerrinton & Son, 1854.

Poems on Miscellaneous Subjects. Philadelphia: Merrrihew & Son, 1857.

Poems on Miscellaneous Subjects. 20th Edition. Philadelphia: Merrihew & Son, 1871.

Sketches of Southern Life. Philadelphia: Merrihew & Son, 1872.

Sketches of Southern Life. Philadelphia: Ferguson, 1888.

Sketches of Southern Life. Philadelphia: Ferguson, 1896.

The Sparrow's Fall and Other Poems. n.d.

Library of Congress Listings

Atlanta Offering: Poems. Philadelphia: Ferguson, 1895.

Idylls of the Bible. Philadelphia: 1006 Bainbridge Street, 1901.

Moses: A Story of the Nile. Philadelphia: Merrihew & Son, 1869.

Moses: A Story of the Nile. Second Edition. Philadelphia: 1006 Bainbridge Street, 1889.

Poems. Philadelphia: Merrihew & Son, 1871. (Cover: Providence: Crawford & Greene, 1876.)

Poems. Philadelphia: Ferguson, 1895.

Poems. Philadelphia: 1900.

Poems on Miscellaneous Subjects. Boston: J. B. Yerrinton & Son, 1854.

Poems on Miscellaneous Subjects. Philadelphia, 1854.

Poems on Miscellaneous Subjects. Second Edition. Boston: J. B. Yerrinton & Son, 1855.

Poems on Miscellaneous Subjects. Second Series. Philadelphia, 1855.

Poems on Miscellaneous Subjects. Ten Thousand. Philadelphia: Merrihew & Son, 1857.

Poems on Miscellaneous Subjects. Second Series. Philadelphia: Merrihew & Son, 1864.

Sketches of Southern Life. Philadelphia, 1872.

Sketches of Southern Life. Philadelphia: Merrihew & Son, 1873.

Sketches of Southern Life. Philadelphia: Merrihew & Son, 1887.

Sketches of Southern Life. Philadelphia: Ferguson, 1888.

Sketches of Southern Life. Philadelphia: Ferguson, 1891.

The Sparrow's Fall and Other Poems. N.p., n.d.

Moorland-Spingarn Collection, Howard University

Atlanta Offering: Poems. Philadelphia: Ferguson, 1895.

Idylls of the Bible. Philadelphia: 1006 Bainbridge Street, 1901.

Moses: A Story of the Nile. Second Edition. Philadelphia: Merrihew & Son, 1869.

Moses: A Story of the Nile. Second Edition. Philadelphia: 1006 Bainbridge Street, 1889.

Poems. Philadelphia: Merrihew & Son, 1871. (Cover: Providence: Crawford & Greene, 1880)

Poems. Philadelphia: 1006 Bainbridge Street, 1896.

Poems. Philadelphia: 1006 Bainbridge Street, 1898.

Poems. Philadelphia: 1006 Bainbridge Street, 1900. Contains six additional poems not indexed.

Poems on Miscellaneous Subjects. Boston: J. B. Yerrinton & Son, 1854.

Poems on Miscellaneous Subjects. 20th Edition. Philadelphia: Merrihew & Son, 1874.

Sketches of Southern Life. Philadelphia: Ferguson, 1891.

Sketches of Southern Life. Philadelphia: Merrihew & Son, 1888. (Cover: Ferguson, 1887)

Sketches of Southern Life. Philadelphia: Ferguson, 1896.

The Sparrow's Fall and Other Poems. n.d.